New Testament Take-Home Bible Stories

Easy-to-Make, Reproducible Mini-Books That Children Can Make and Keep

by
Thomas C. Ewald

**Illustrations by
Joni Oeltjenbruns**

Carson-Dellosa Christian Publishing

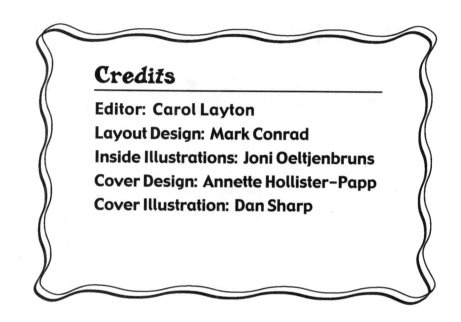

Credits

Editor: Carol Layton
Layout Design: Mark Conrad
Inside Illustrations: Joni Oeltjenbruns
Cover Design: Annette Hollister–Papp
Cover Illustration: Dan Sharp

ISBN 0-88724-872-1

Table of Contents

About This Book

New Testament Take-Home Bible Stories contains 62 stories for children to color and make into their very own story books! The last page of each book contains a question about the story and a Scripture reference to one of the key verses of the story. Use this reference to teach children how to locate passages in their Bibles, and then read the story to them. Reading from the Bible is an excellent way to teach the story and to enrich children's hearts and minds with the beauty and power of the Living Word. Making the take-home book is a fun and interactive way to supplement this Bible reading. (The captions in the take-home books are paraphrases rather than direct quotations from Scripture.) As you discuss the application questions, lead children to understand that the God of the Bible—the God of Peter, Mary Magdalene, and Paul—is also their God. He desires to fellowship with them, provide for them, and deliver them just as He has always done for His people. He is the same yesterday, today, and forever!

How to Make the Take-Home Books

You may choose to remove the pages (1a), or make copies directly from the book (1b).

1a. To remove pages: Carefully separate the page along the perforation. To reduce the risk of tearing, score the perforation first with a craft knife or a scissors tip. Align the page with the guides on the copy machine, making sure to place the perforated side away from any edge on the machine. Make single-sided copies of the page on standard 8¹/₂" x 11" paper.

1b. To copy directly from book: Open the book and place it as flat as possible on the copy machine and make single-sided copies on standard 8¹/₂" x 11" paper.

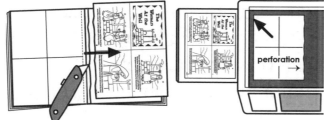

2. Trim the edge close to where the perforation was (if following 1b). Cut apart the mini-book pages along the solid lines. Each book will have 8 pages (including the cover).

3. Put the pages in order with the cover on top. Staple the pages on the left side to make the book. (Depending on age level, it may be easier to color the illustrations before the books are assembled.)

Speechless!

Gabriel told Zechariah that his wife Elizabeth was going to have a baby named John. He would grow up and tell everyone that Jesus was coming.

2

Zechariah was serving in the temple, when suddenly—the angel Gabriel appeared!

1

Zechariah was amazed. He asked Gabriel how he could be sure it would happen.

3

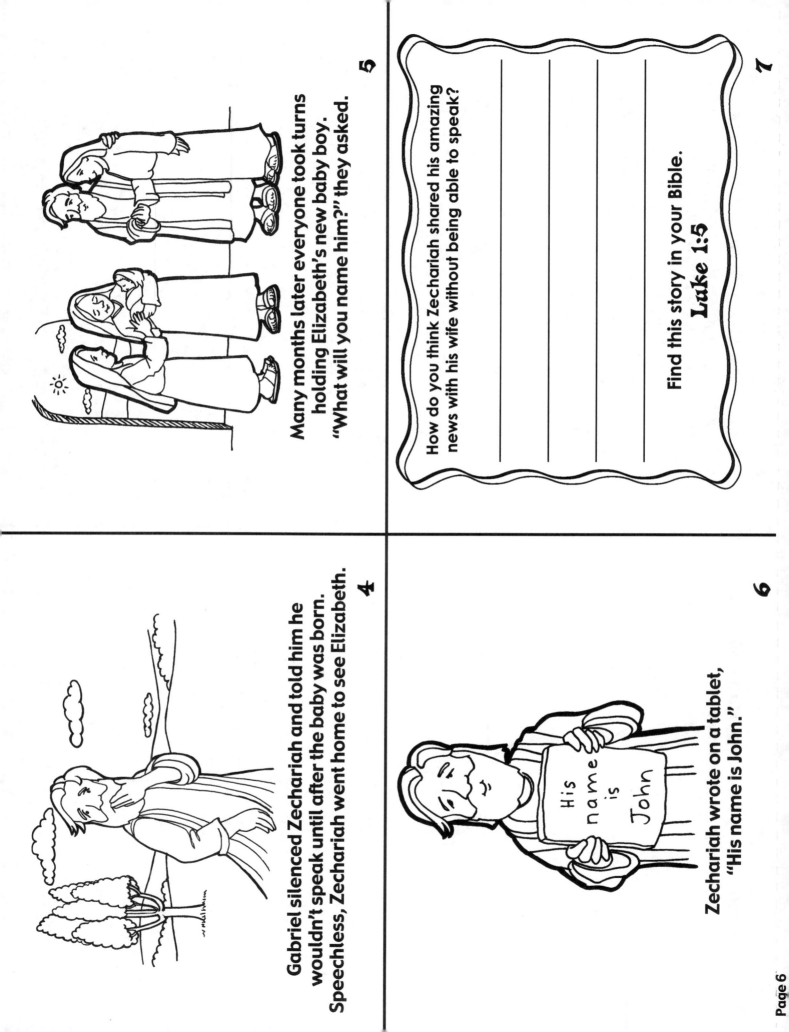

5

Many months later everyone took turns holding Elizabeth's new baby boy. "What will you name him?" they asked.

7

How do you think Zechariah shared his amazing news with his wife without being able to speak?

_____

_____

_____

_____

Find this story in your Bible.
Luke 1:5

4

Gabriel silenced Zechariah and told him he wouldn't speak until after the baby was born. Speechless, Zechariah went home to see Elizabeth.

6

His name is John

Zechariah wrote on a tablet, "His name is John."

An Angel with Good News!

"But I'm just a young woman. What news could God have for me?"

2

The angel Gabriel visited Mary at her house. He told her he had big news for her.

1

Gabriel told her that God was going to make her the mother of a special child who would grow up and save God's people.

3

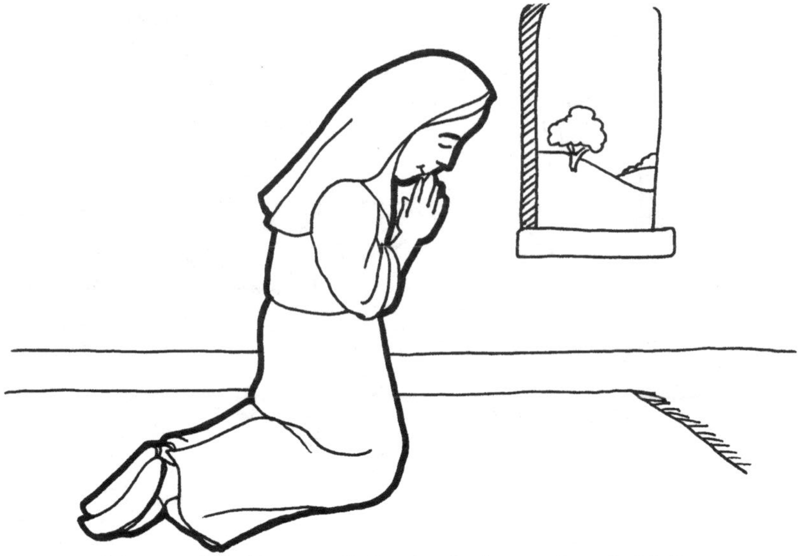

Gabriel told Mary she was blessed.

5

What do you think Mary named her baby?

Find this story in your Bible.
Luke 1:26

7

Mary believed Gabriel and told him she would do whatever God asked.

4

Soon Mary found out that she was about to have a baby.

6

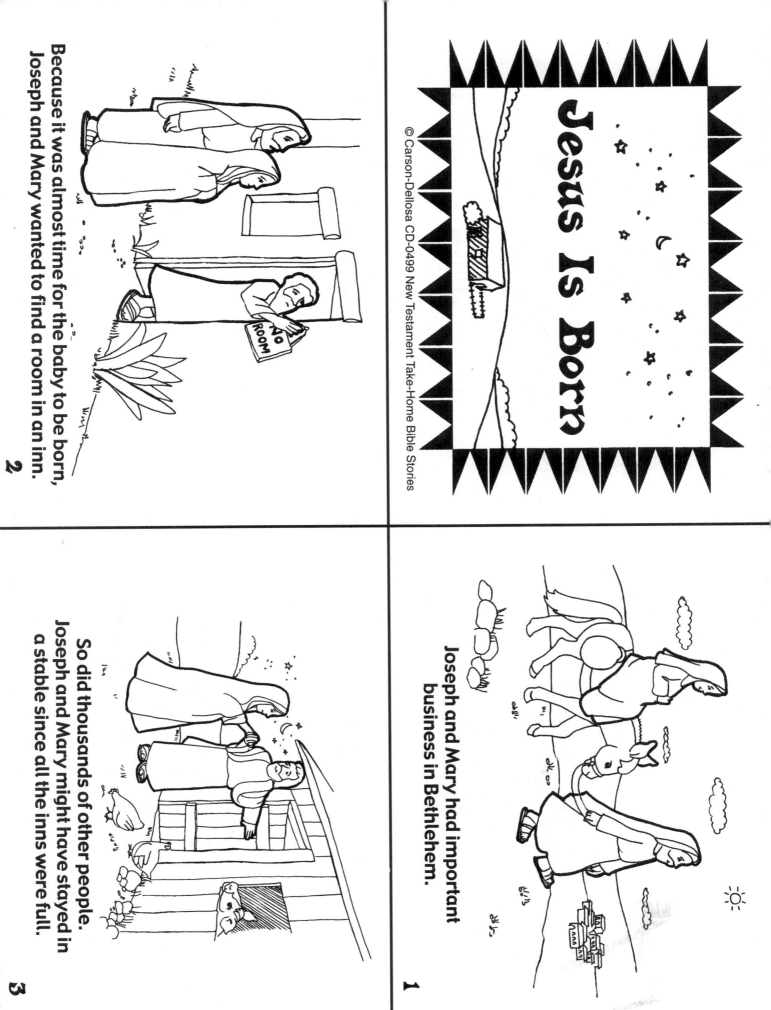

Jesus Is Born

Because it was almost time for the baby to be born, Joseph and Mary wanted to find a room in an inn.

2

Joseph and Mary had important business in Bethlehem.

1

So did thousands of other people. Joseph and Mary might have stayed in a stable since all the inns were full.

3

She wrapped Him in warm cloths and put Him in a manger.

5

What are stables normally used for?

Find this story in your Bible.
Luke 2:1

7

There, under a starry sky, Mary gave birth to her child.

4

Shepherds came to visit the Holy Family.

6

Angels and Shepherds

An angel appeared and said, "Don't be afraid, I have great news! A Savior has been born in Bethlehem."

2

On a night just like any other, shepherds sat watching over their flocks.

1

Just then, other angels appeared and said, "Glory to God in the highest!"

3

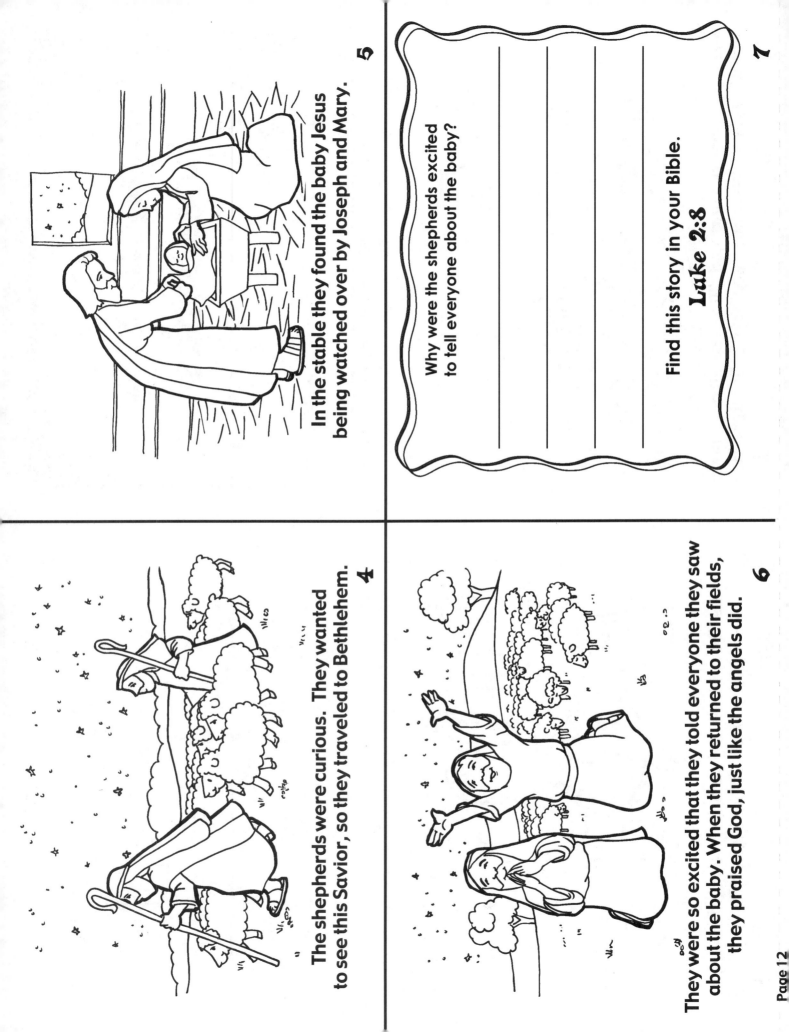

5

In the stable they found the baby Jesus being watched over by Joseph and Mary.

7

Why were the shepherds excited to tell everyone about the baby?

Find this story in your Bible.
Luke 2:8

4

The shepherds were curious. They wanted to see this Savior, so they traveled to Bethlehem.

6

They were so excited that they told everyone they saw about the baby. When they returned to their fields, they praised God, just like the angels did.

Simeon's Prayer

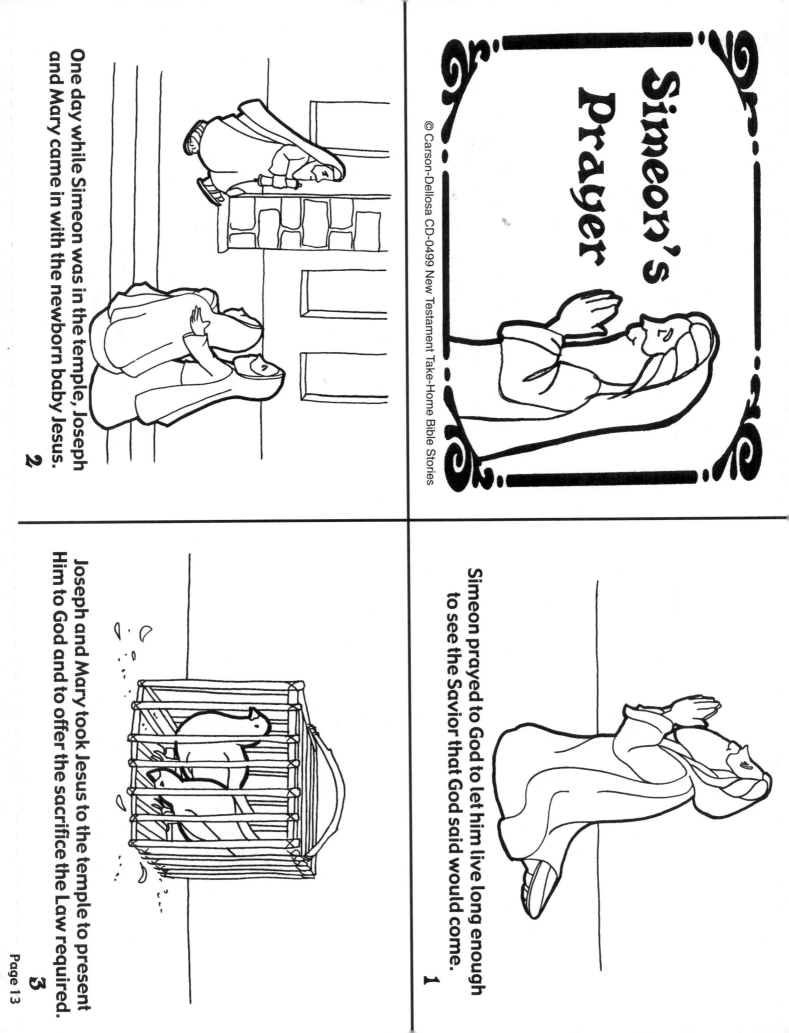

One day while Simeon was in the temple, Joseph and Mary came in with the newborn baby Jesus.

2

Simeon prayed to God to let him live long enough to see the Savior that God said would come.

1

Joseph and Mary took Jesus to the temple to present Him to God and to offer the sacrifice the Law required.

3

5

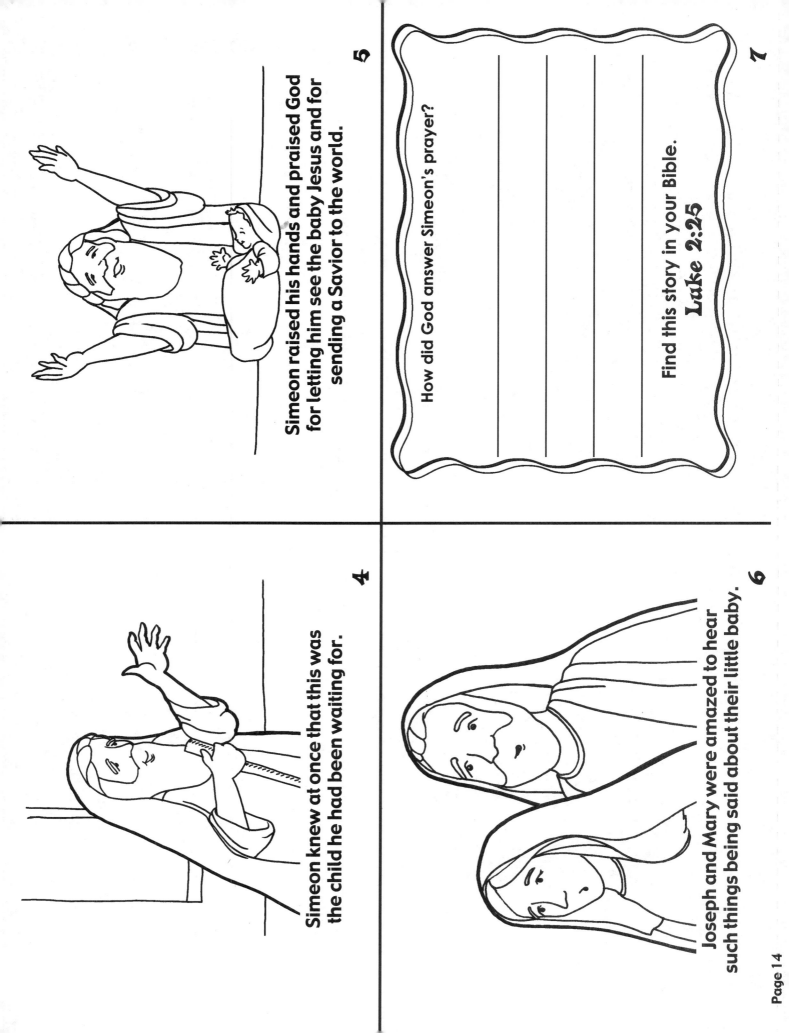

Simeon raised his hands and praised God for letting him see the baby Jesus and for sending a Savior to the world.

7

How did God answer Simeon's prayer?

Find this story in your Bible.
Luke 2:25

4

Simeon knew at once that this was the child he had been waiting for.

6

Joseph and Mary were amazed to hear such things being said about their little baby.

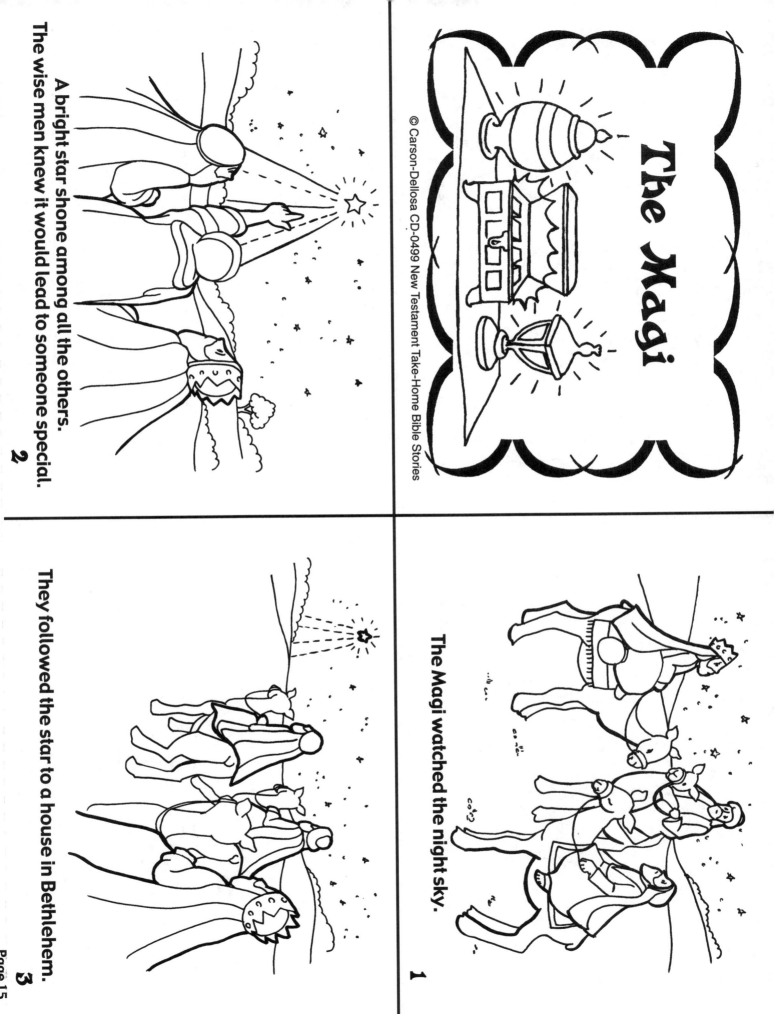

The Magi

A bright star shone among all the others. The wise men knew it would lead to someone special.

2

The Magi watched the night sky.

1

They followed the star to a house in Bethlehem.

3

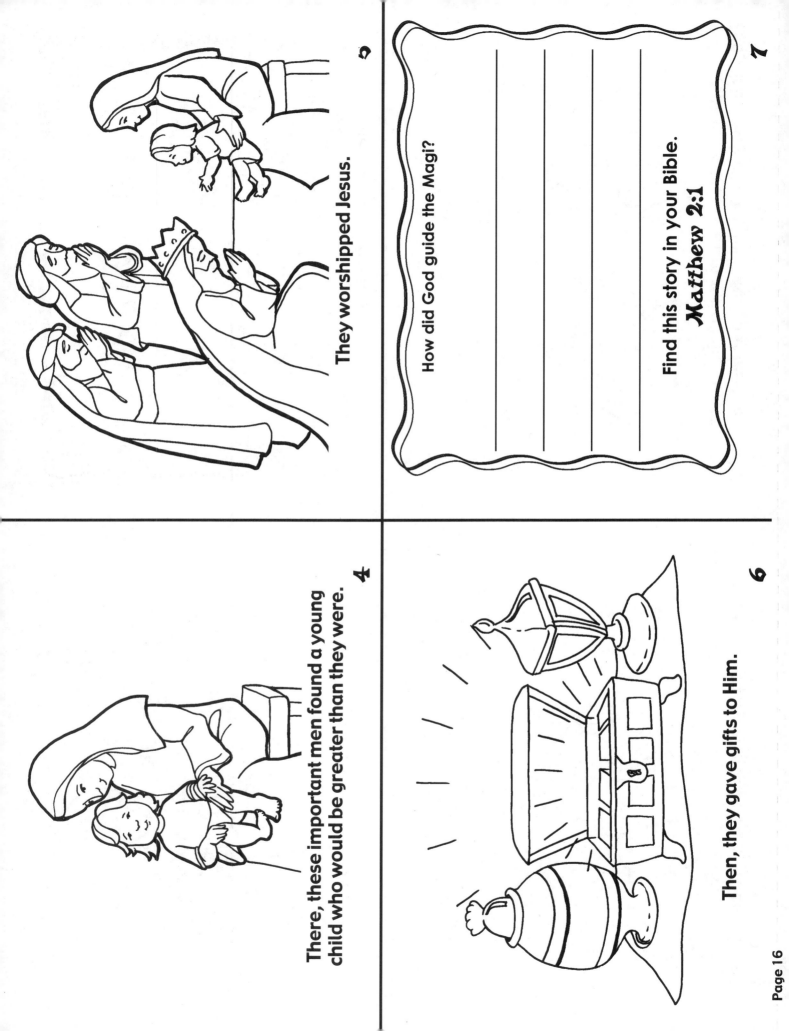

5

They worshipped Jesus.

7

How did God guide the Magi?

Find this story in your Bible.
Matthew 2:1

4

There, these important men found a young child who would be greater than they were.

6

Then, they gave gifts to Him.

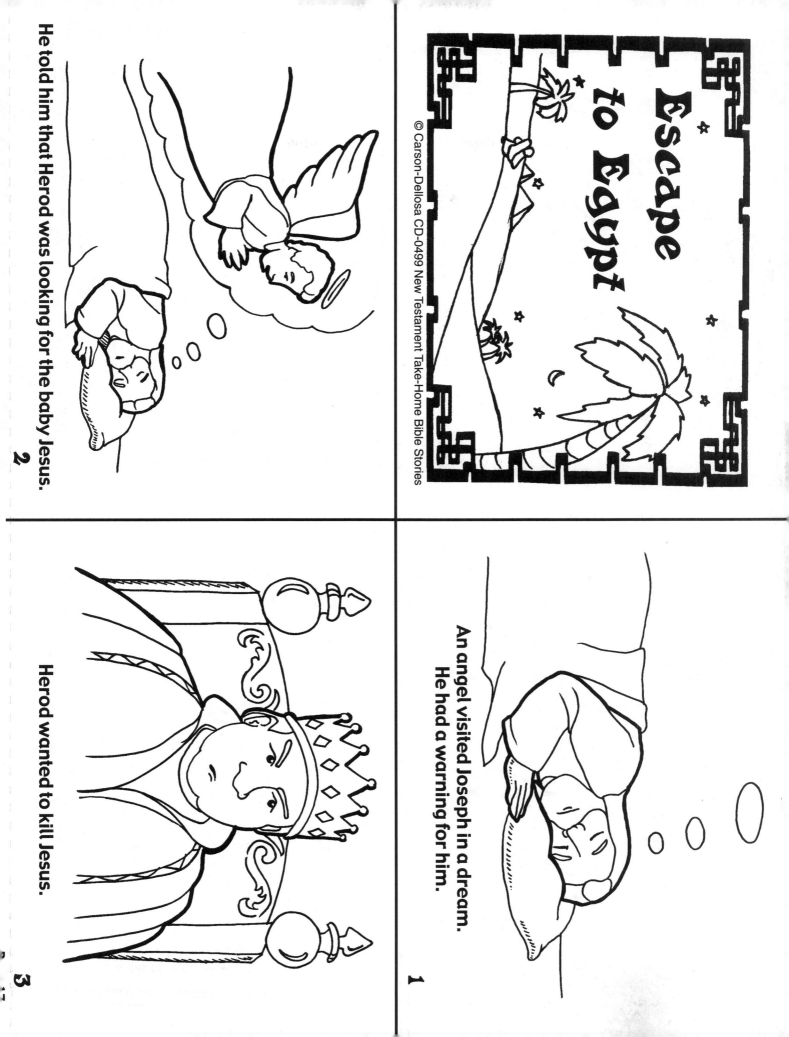

He told him that Herod was looking for the baby Jesus.

2

Escape to Egypt

An angel visited Joseph in a dream. He had a warning for him.

1

Herod wanted to kill Jesus.

3

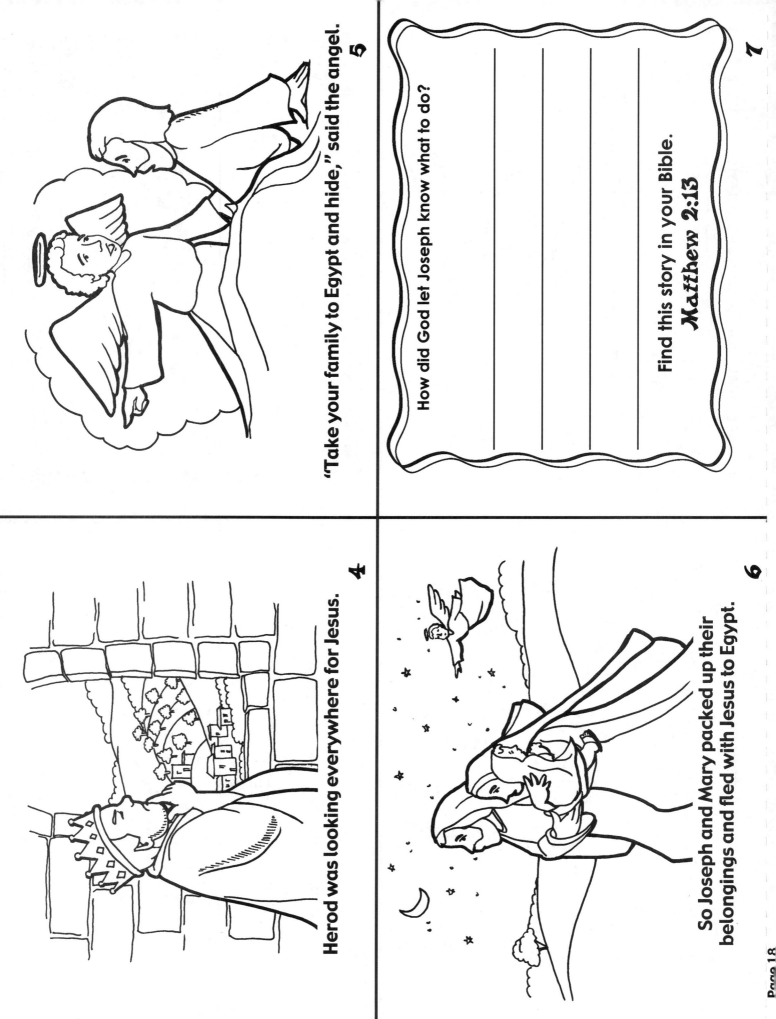

5

"Take your family to Egypt and hide," said the angel.

7

How did God let Joseph know what to do?

Find this story in your Bible. *Matthew 2:13*

4

Herod was looking everywhere for Jesus.

6

So Joseph and Mary packed up their belongings and fled with Jesus to Egypt.

Jesus in the Temple

The city was so crowded! It seemed like everyone was there.

2

When Jesus was a young boy, His parents took Him to Jerusalem to celebrate Passover.

1

When the celebration was over, Joseph and Mary started home. They noticed Jesus was missing. "I thought you had Him!" "I thought YOU did!"

3

5

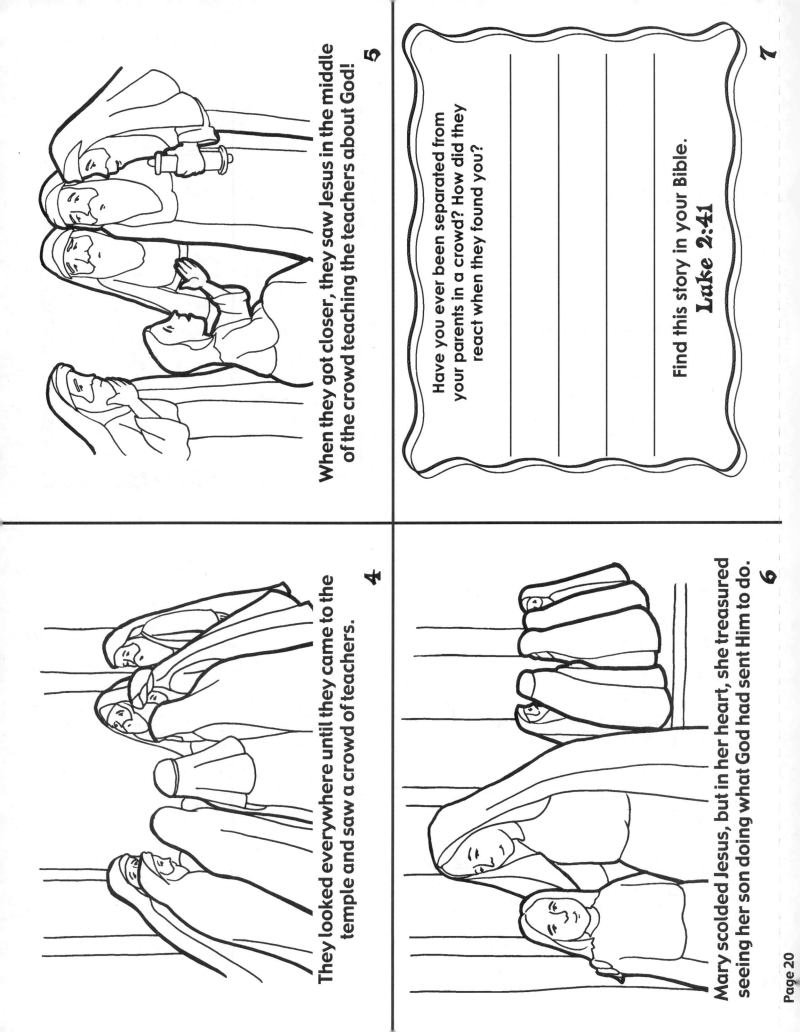

When they got closer, they saw Jesus in the middle of the crowd teaching the teachers about God!

7

Have you ever been separated from your parents in a crowd? How did they react when they found you?

_____

_____

_____

_____

Find this story in your Bible.
Luke 2:41

4

They looked everywhere until they came to the temple and saw a crowd of teachers.

6

Mary scolded Jesus, but in her heart, she treasured seeing her son doing what God had sent Him to do.

He preached to people—telling them to stop doing bad things because the Savior was coming.

2

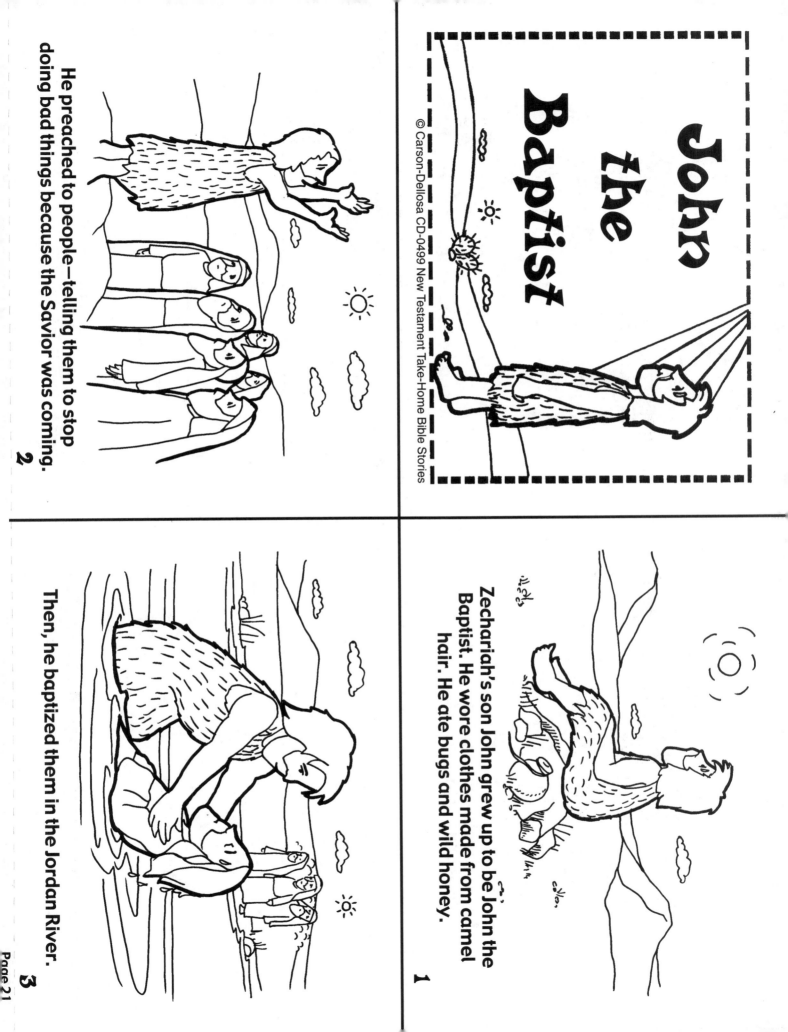

John
the
Baptist

Zechariah's son John grew up to be John the Baptist. He wore clothes made from camel hair. He ate bugs and wild honey.

1

Then, he baptized them in the Jordan River.

3

5

Some people thought that John was the Savior.

7

What was John's message to the people?

Find this story in your Bible.
Matthew 3:1

4

Some people yelled at him because they did not like his message.

6

John always told them, "I am not the Savior. I am not even good enough to carry His sandals."

The Baptism of Jesus

© Carson-Dellosa CD-0499 New Testament Take-Home Bible Stories

He told everybody, "Look, this is the Savior!" Jesus said, "I have come to be baptized."

2

John said, "I cannot baptize you! You are the Savior!"

3

One day when John was baptizing people, Jesus drew near.

1

So John baptized Jesus in the Jordan River.

5

Why did John agree to baptize Jesus?

Find this story in your Bible.
Matthew 3:13

7

But Jesus explained that it is what God wanted.

4

Just then, the Holy Spirit came down like a dove from heaven and lighted on Jesus. A voice said, "This is my son. I am proud of Him."

6

The Tempter Loses

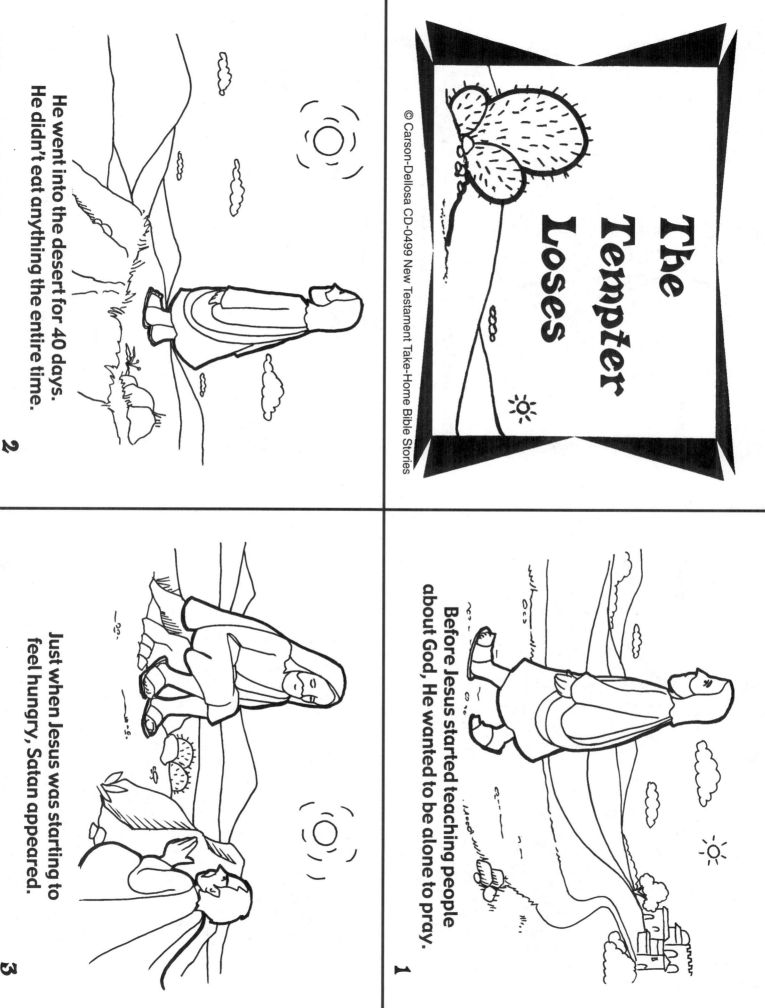

He went into the desert for 40 days. He didn't eat anything the entire time.

2

Before Jesus started teaching people about God, He wanted to be alone to pray.

1

Just when Jesus was starting to feel hungry, Satan appeared.

3

5

Jesus told Satan that the Bible says to worship only God. Jesus spoke God's Word to Satan.

7

What weapon did Jesus use against Satan?

Find this story in your Bible.
Matthew 4:1

4

Satan offered Jesus bread, but Jesus said, "no." Satan offered to give Jesus some of his authority on the earth, but Jesus said, "no."

6

Jesus told Satan to leave and he did. Angels came and took care of Jesus.

Jesus Chooses His Disciples

He found some men fishing.
They were not catching anything.

2

Jesus wanted people to go with
Him as He taught about God.

1

Jesus told them to put their net
on the other side of the boat.

3

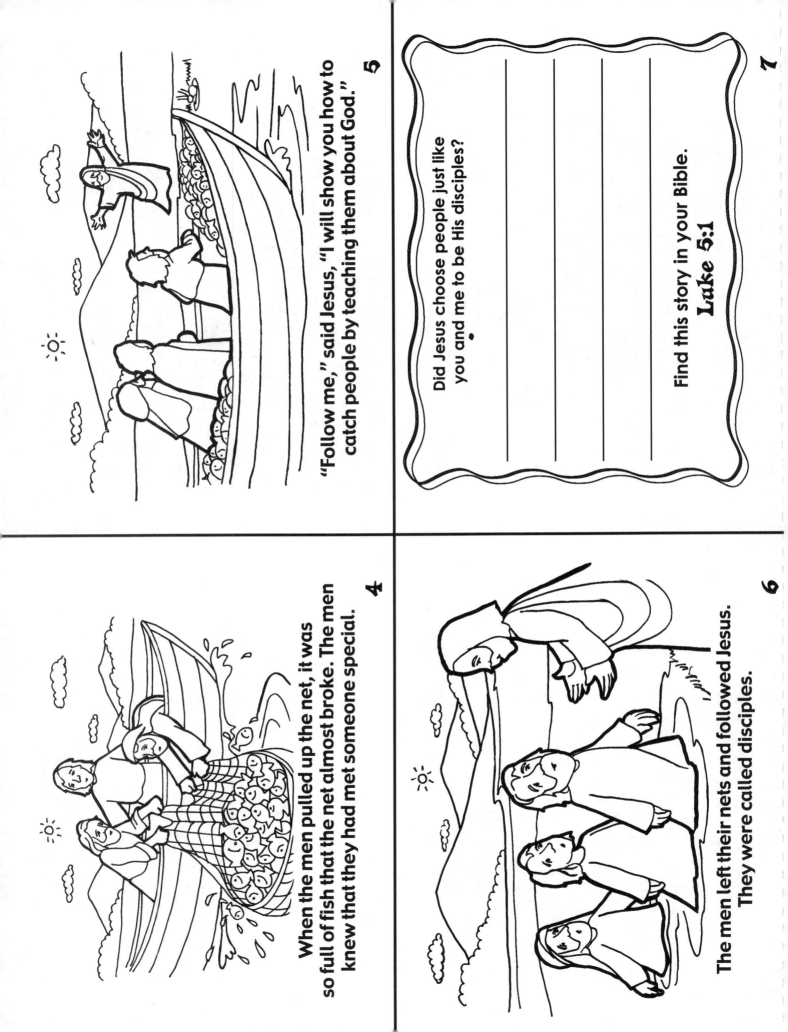

5

"Follow me," said Jesus, "I will show you how to catch people by teaching them about God."

7

Did Jesus choose people just like you and me to be His disciples?

_____

_____

_____

_____

Find this story in your Bible.
Luke 5:1

4

When the men pulled up the net, it was so full of fish that the net almost broke. The men knew that they had met someone special.

6

The men left their nets and followed Jesus. They were called disciples.

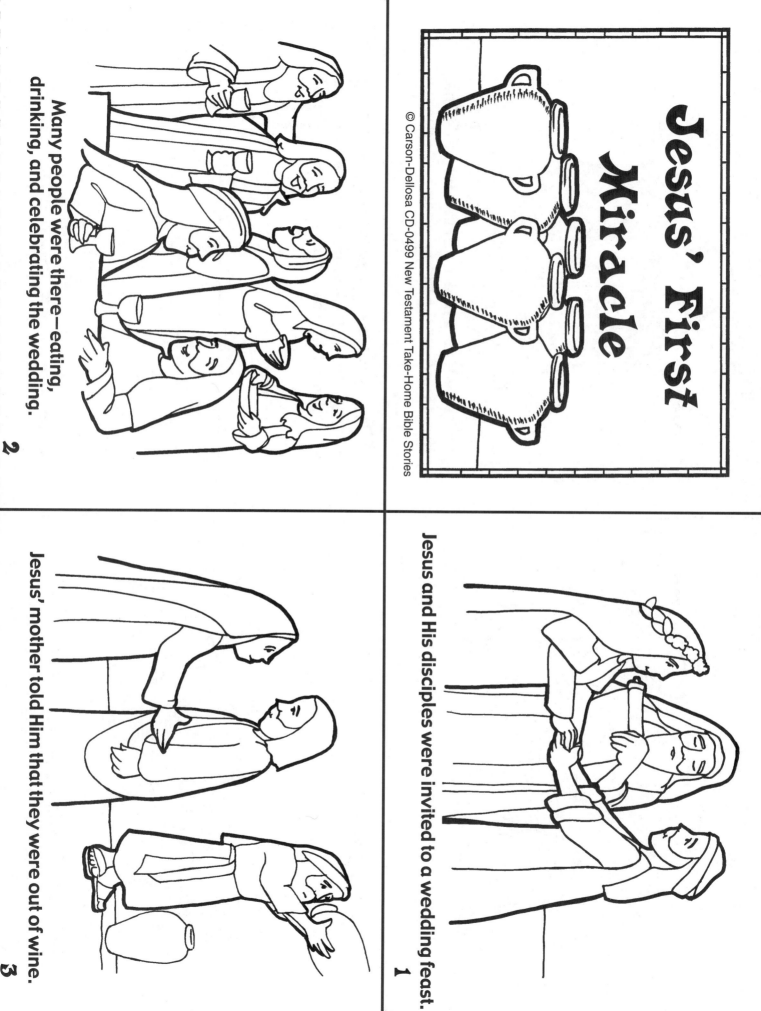

Jesus' First Miracle

Many people were there—eating, drinking, and celebrating the wedding.

2

Jesus' mother told Him that they were out of wine.

3

Jesus and His disciples were invited to a wedding feast.

1

When they poured the water into cups, they found out that it had been turned into wine.

5

How do you think Jesus' mother felt when when Jesus turned the water into wine at the wedding?

Find this story in your Bible.
John 2:1

7

Jesus told them to fill six big jars with water.

4

The servants were amazed.
This was the first miracle Jesus performed.

6

As they got closer, they saw that the noise was from people selling animals and exchanging money.

2

Jesus Clears the Temple

© Carson-Dellosa CD-0499 New Testament Take-Home Bible Stories

Jesus drove the sheep and cattle out with a whip, pushed the money tables over, and told the sellers of doves, "Get those out of here!"

3

Jesus and His disciples heard a noise coming from the temple.

1

5

Some people thought this was wrong for Jesus to do.

7

Why did Jesus make the sellers leave the temple?

_____

_____

_____

_____

Find this story in your Bible.
John 2:12

4

Jesus told the people, "This temple is for praying and for worshipping God. You have turned it into a place to make money!"

6

Others, like His disciples, knew this was a sign that Jesus was God's son.

He waited until it was dark to find Jesus.

2

A Midnight Meeting

He asked Jesus what he needed to do to go to heaven.

3

Nicodemus wanted to learn more about Jesus. But he was afraid of what the other teachers would think if they saw him talking to Jesus.

1

Nicodemus thought Jesus meant that he had to become like a baby again.

5

What did Jesus say we must do to go to heaven?

_____

_____

_____

_____

Find this story in your Bible.
John 3:1

7

Jesus told Nicodemus, "You must be born again."

4

But Jesus explained that being born again means believing that Jesus is the Son of God.

6

The Woman at the Well

A woman came to the well. Jesus told her that God was like a never-ending supply of living water.

2

Jesus and the disciples had been traveling. Jesus stopped at a well while the disciples went to find food.

1

The woman told Jesus that she was a bad person. She did not feel good enough to be loved by God.

3

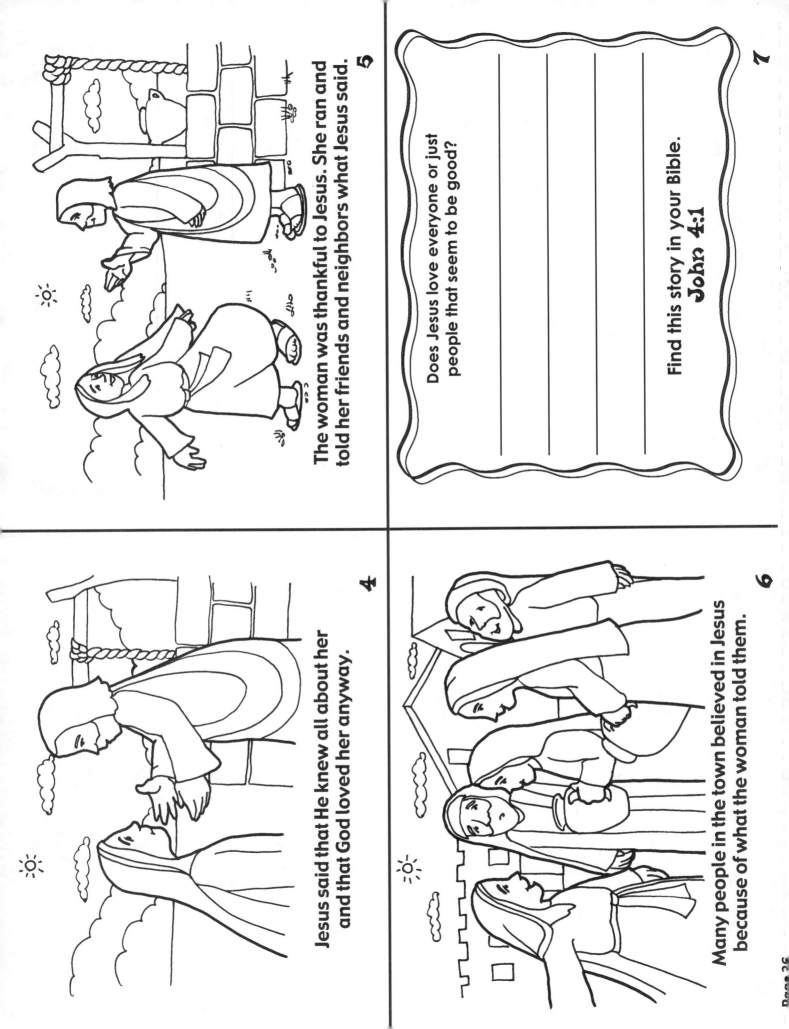

The woman was thankful to Jesus. She ran and told her friends and neighbors what Jesus said.

5

Does Jesus love everyone or just people that seem to be good?

Find this story in your Bible. **John 4:1**

7

Jesus said that He knew all about her and that God loved her anyway.

4

Many people in the town believed in Jesus because of what the woman told them.

6

He said weak people would be made strong . . .

2

Sermon on the Mount

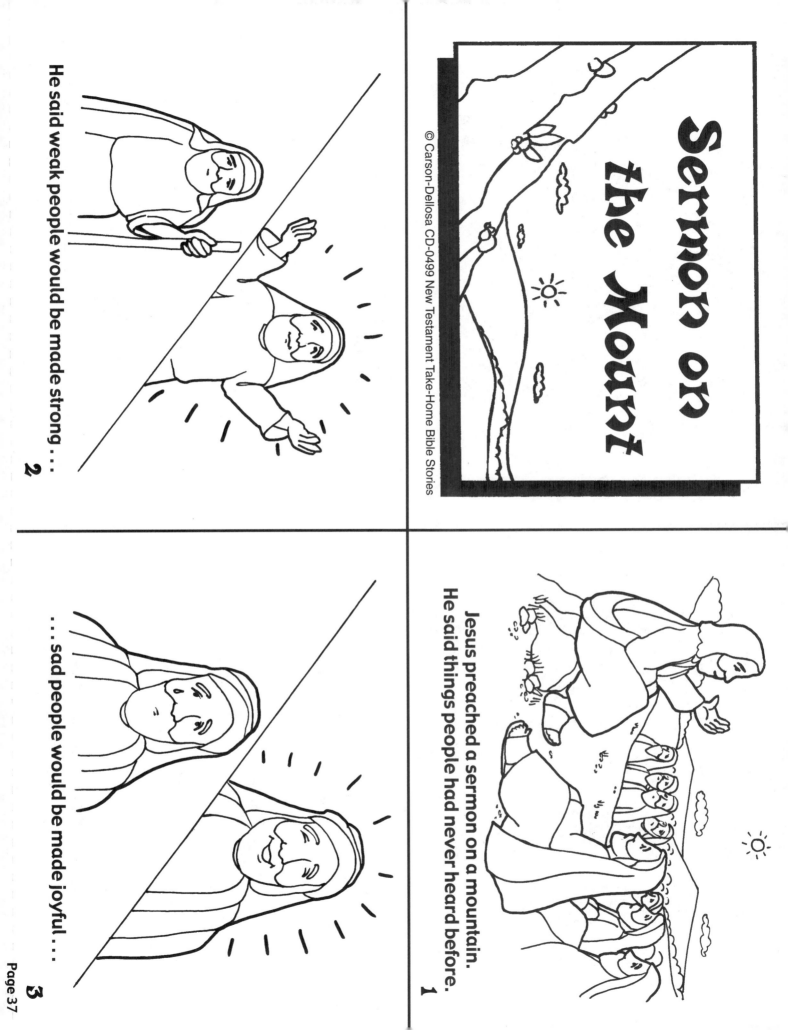

. . . sad people would be made joyful . . .

3

Jesus preached a sermon on a mountain.
He said things people had never heard before.

1

5

. . . and hungry people would be filled.

7

How has Jesus changed your life?

_____

_____

_____

_____

Find this story in your Bible.
Matthew 5:1

4

. . . poor people would be made rich . . . .

6

He said that this is what life is like
for people in God's Kingdom.

The Sower and the Seed

Sometimes, when people gathered around Jesus, He would compare things in nature to spiritual things.

1

He wanted to explain to people the importance of hearing God's Word and doing what it says.

HOLY BIBLE

2

He told about a farmer planting seeds. Some seeds fell on rocks and didn't grow.

3

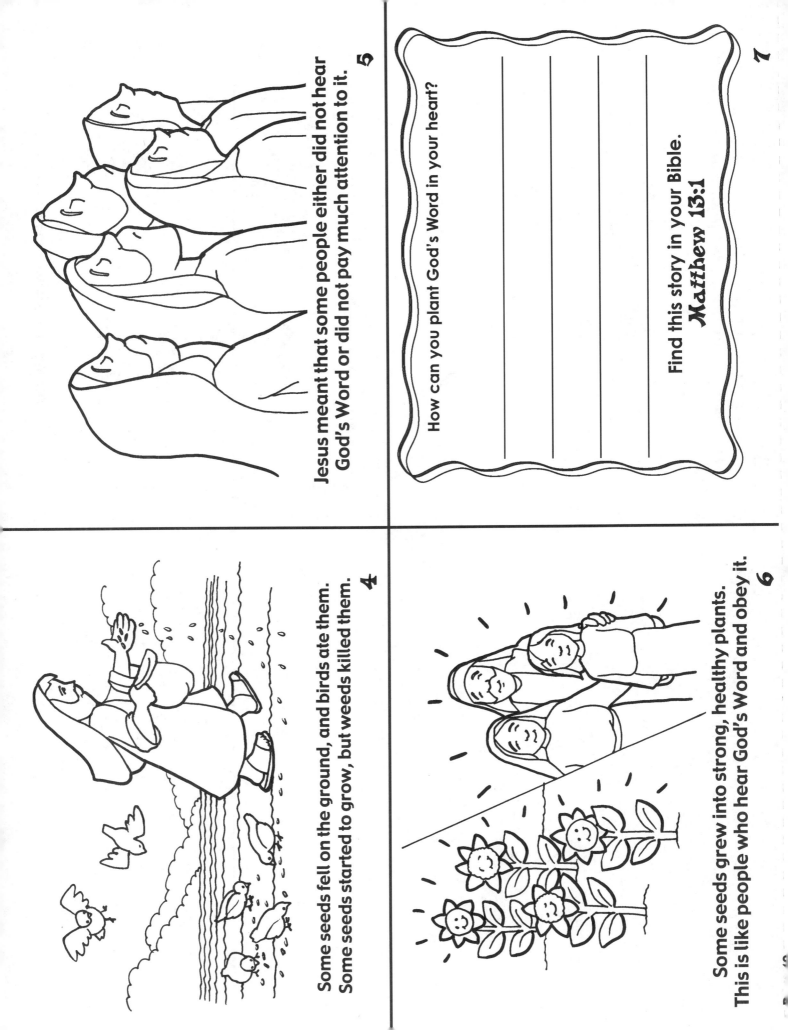

Jesus meant that some people either did not hear God's Word or did not pay much attention to it.

5

How can you plant God's Word in your heart?

Find this story in your Bible.
Matthew 13:1

7

Some seeds fell on the ground, and birds ate them. Some seeds started to grow, but weeds killed them.

4

Some seeds grew into strong, healthy plants. This is like people who hear God's Word and obey it.

6

5,000+ Fish Dinners

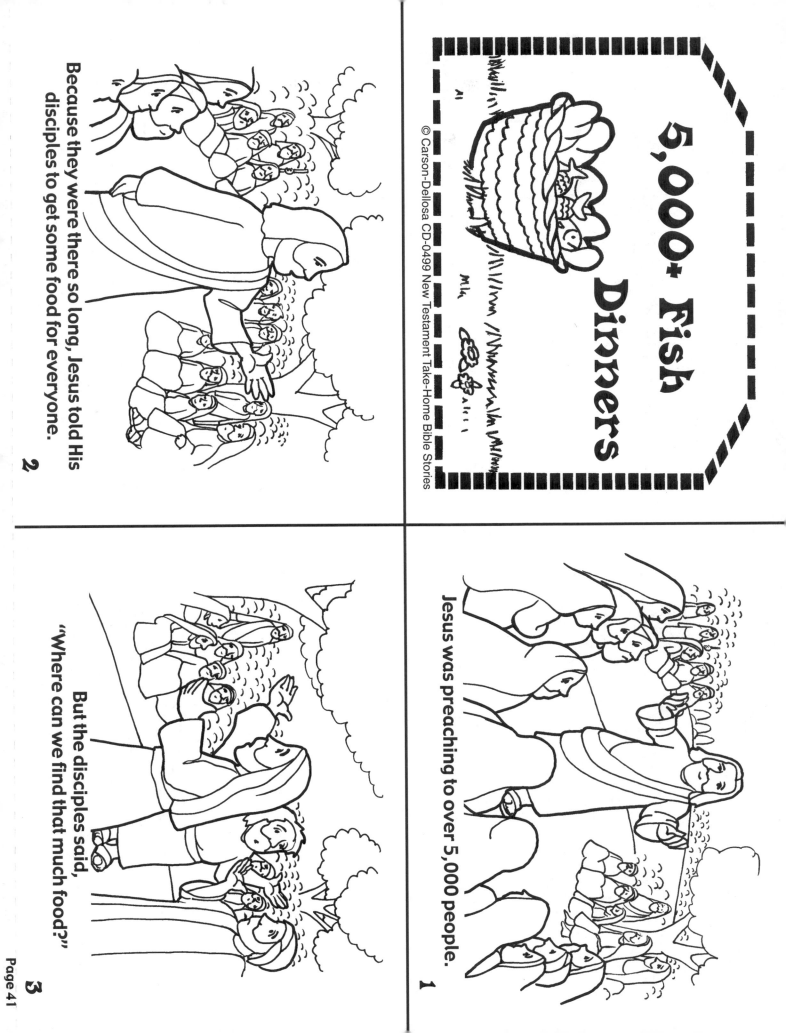

Because they were there so long, Jesus told His disciples to get some food for everyone.

2

But the disciples said, "Where can we find that much food?"

3

Jesus was preaching to over 5,000 people.

1

5

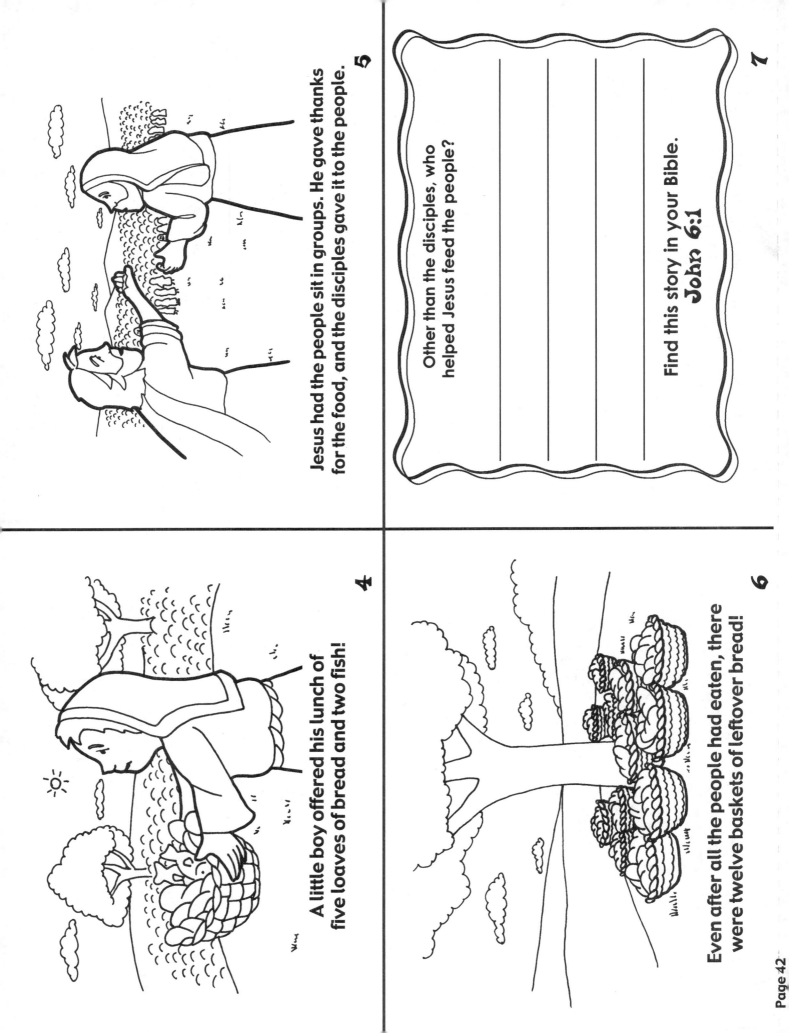

Jesus had the people sit in groups. He gave thanks for the food, and the disciples gave it to the people.

7

Other than the disciples, who helped Jesus feed the people?

_____

_____

_____

_____

Find this story in your Bible.
John 6:1

4

A little boy offered his lunch of five loaves of bread and two fish!

6

Even after all the people had eaten, there were twelve baskets of leftover bread!

Walking on Water

They saw Jesus coming to them—walking on the water. They thought He was a ghost. He said, "Don't be afraid, it is I, Jesus."

2

Peter told Jesus he wanted to walk on water. He got out of the boat.

3

The disciples were rowing across the lake when big waves started to make the boat bounce around.

1

5

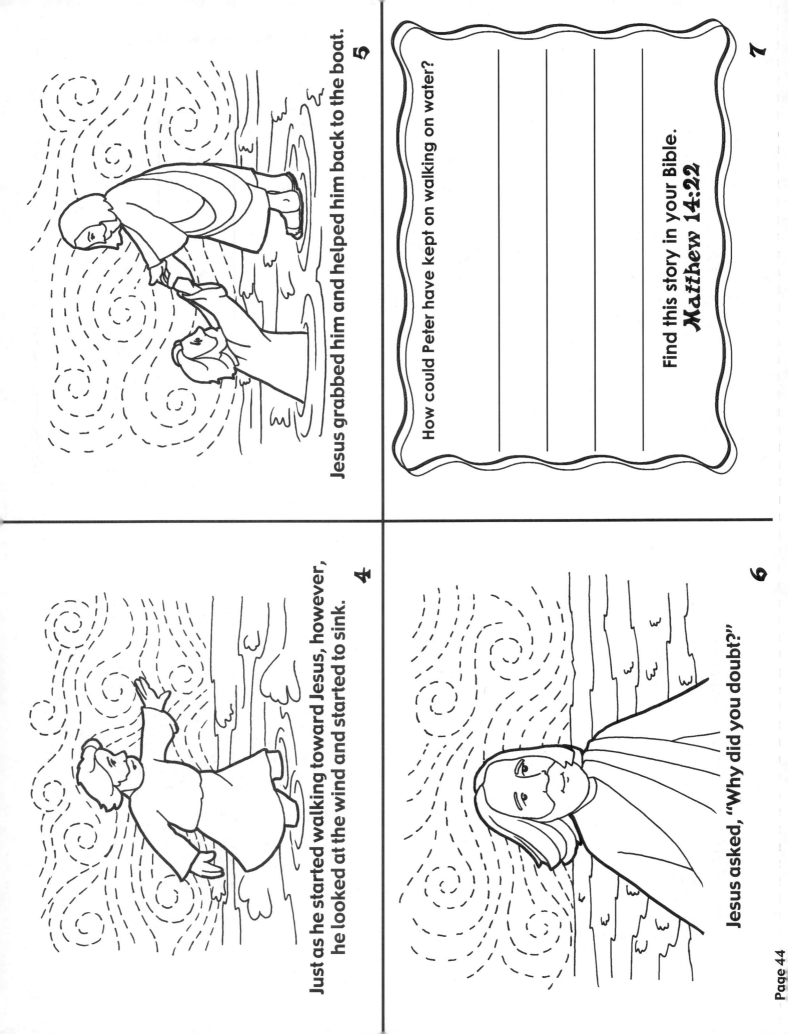

Jesus grabbed him and helped him back to the boat.

7

How could Peter have kept on walking on water?

_____

_____

_____

_____

Find this story in your Bible.
Matthew 14:22

4

Just as he started walking toward Jesus, however, he looked at the wind and started to sink.

6

Jesus asked, "Why did you doubt?"

He told them, "You are like sheep that need a shepherd."

2

The Good Shepherd

"I am like the shepherd.
I lead you and protect you from harm."

3

People always asked Jesus to tell them who He was.

1

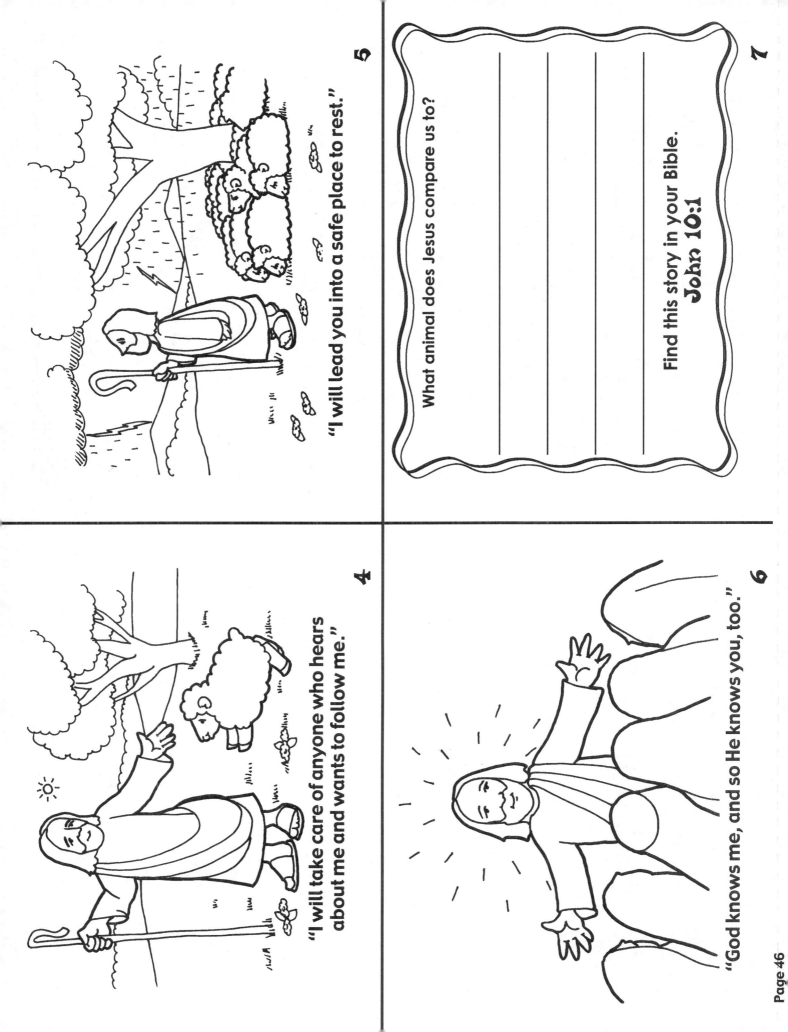

5

"I will lead you into a safe place to rest."

7

What animal does Jesus compare us to?

Find this story in your Bible.
John 10:1

4

"I will take care of anyone who hears about me and wants to follow me."

6

"God knows me, and so He knows you, too."

The Good Samaritan

Some men robbed and beat him and left him in the dirt.

2

Jesus told a story about a man traveling by himself along a road.

1

Two men passed by the man but did not help him.

3

He took him to an inn where he could get better.

5

A Samaritan saw the man and bandaged his wounds.

4

How can you be like the good Samaritan?

Find this story in your Bible.
Luke 10:25

7

Jesus says we should be like this Samaritan and help people who need us, not just pass them by.

6

Mary and Martha

They knew that Jesus was tired from traveling so much.

2

Mary and Martha were friends of Jesus.

1

When He came to their house, they wanted to treat Him very well.

3

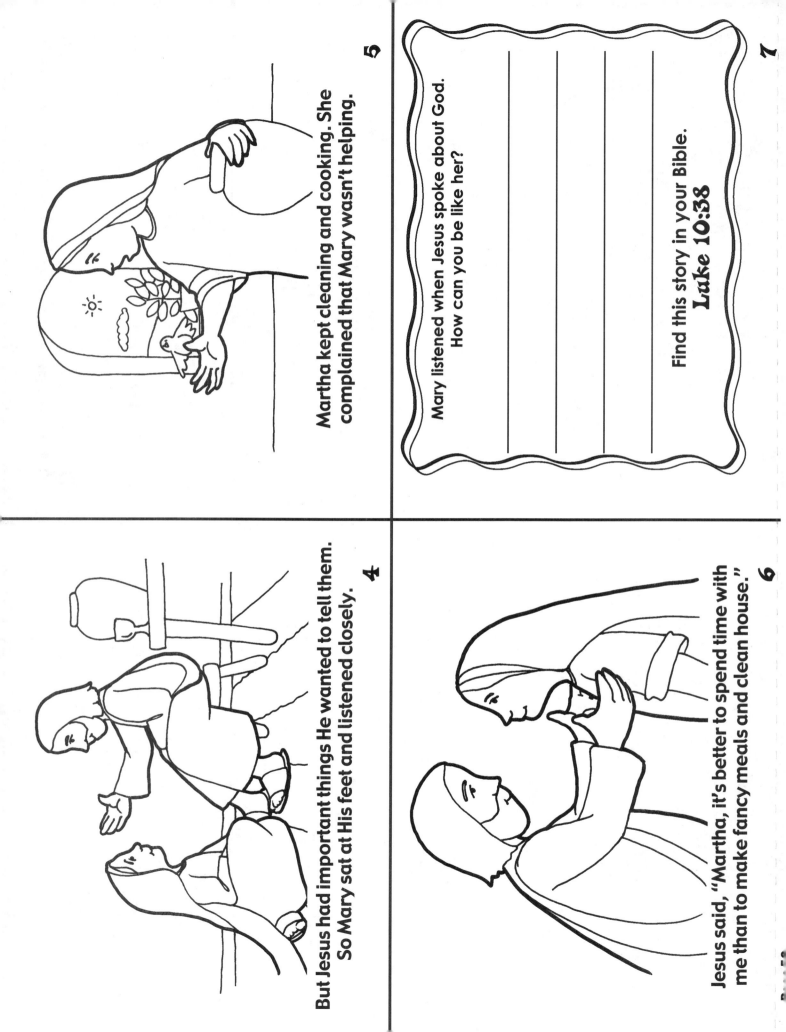

5

Martha kept cleaning and cooking. She complained that Mary wasn't helping.

7

Mary listened when Jesus spoke about God. How can you be like her?

Find this story in your Bible.
Luke 10:38

4

But Jesus had important things He wanted to tell them. So Mary sat at His feet and listened closely.

6

Jesus said, "Martha, it's better to spend time with me than to make fancy meals and clean house."

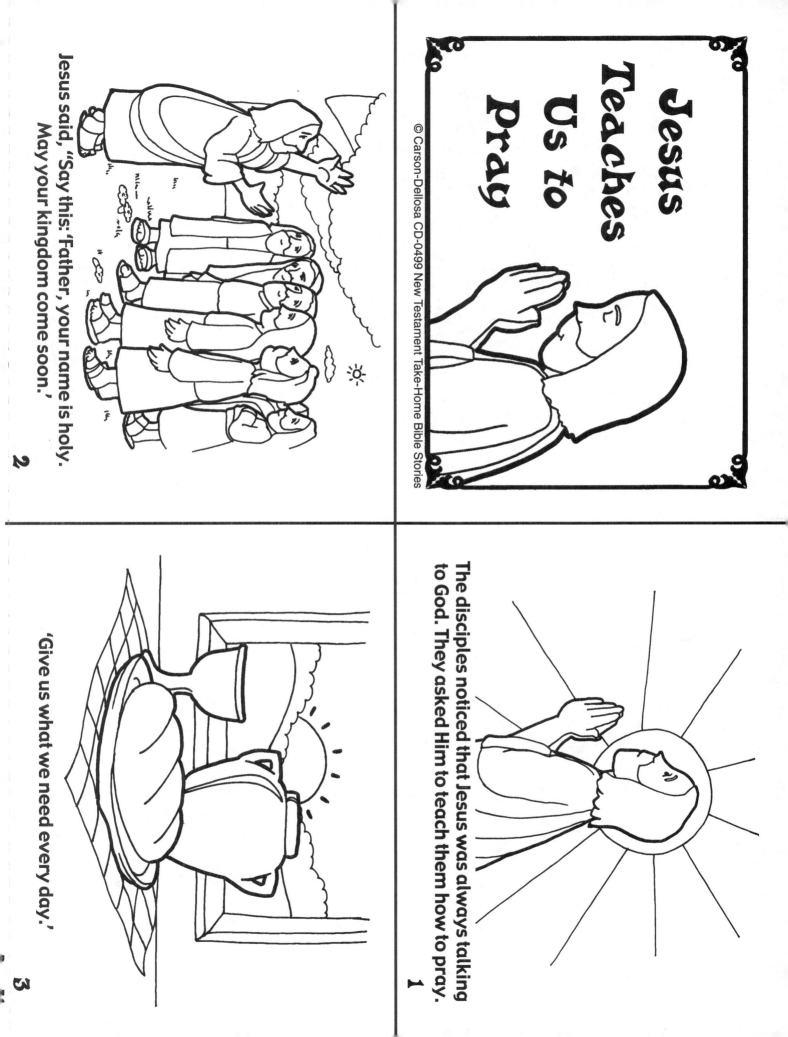

Jesus Teaches Us to Pray

© Carson-Dellosa CD-0499 New Testament Take-Home Bible Stories

Jesus said, "Say this: 'Father, your name is holy. May your kingdom come soon.'

2

The disciples noticed that Jesus was always talking to God. They asked Him to teach them how to pray.

1

'Give us what we need every day.'

3

5

'Keep us away from bad things.'"

7

What does The Lord's Prayer teach us about forgiveness?

Find this story in your Bible. *Luke 11:1*

4

'Forgive us when we do wrong, as we forgive others when they do bad things to us.'

6

the LORD'S PRAYER

Jesus taught His disciples "The Lord's Prayer."

The Lost Sheep

He told about a shepherd with 100 sheep. The shepherd noticed one of the sheep was missing.

2

So the shepherd left the other sheep and looked everywhere for the missing one.

3

Jesus wanted people to know how much God loved them.

1

He put the sheep on his shoulders and carried it all the way home.

What does God do when lost people are saved?

Find this story in your Bible.
Luke 15:1

The shepherd was so excited when he found the lost sheep.

I LOVE YOU

Jesus wants us to know that God rejoices when we come to Him.

The Lost Son

© Carson-Dellosa CD-0499 New Testament Take-Home Bible Stories

Jesus wanted people to know that God loves them even when they sin.

1

He told about a boy who left home to have fun living in the city. He spent all his money on parties.

2

When his money ran out, so did his friends.

3

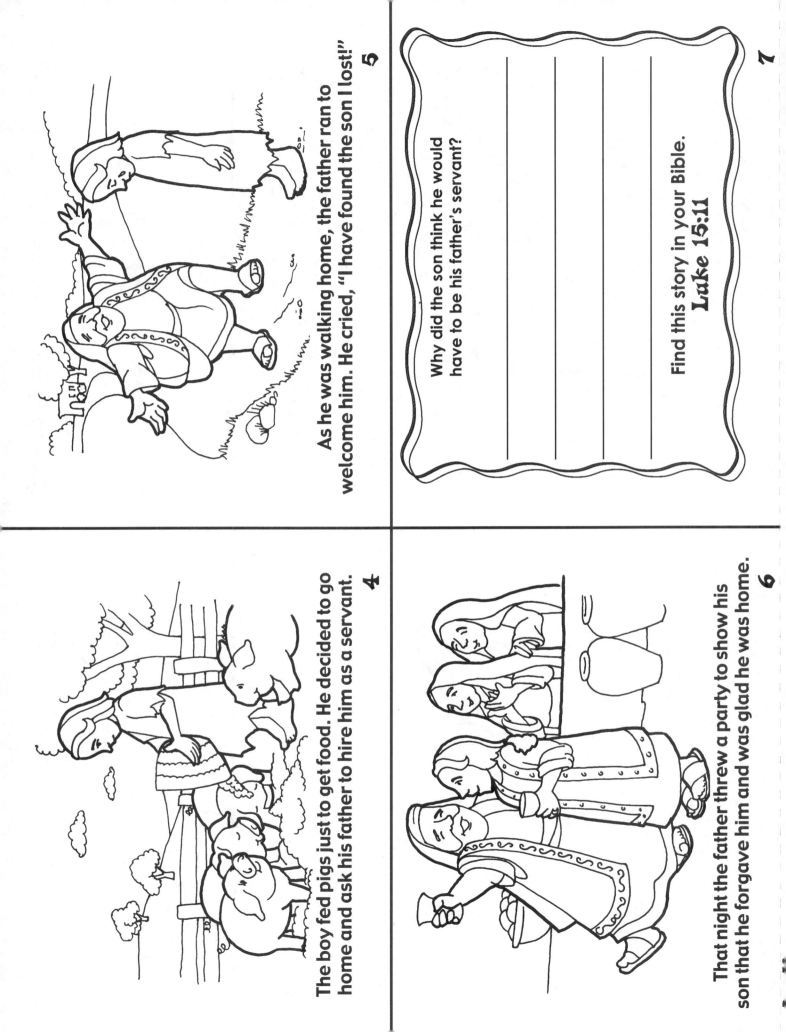

As he was walking home, the father ran to welcome him. He cried, "I have found the son I lost!"

5

Why did the son think he would have to be his father's servant?

_____
_____
_____
_____

Find this story in your Bible.
Luke 15:11

7

The boy fed pigs just to get food. He decided to go home and ask his father to hire him as a servant.

4

That night the father threw a party to show his son that he forgave him and was glad he was home.

6

A Very Important Meeting

A light shone on Jesus. His face was very bright.

2

Jesus and three of His disciples went up a mountain.

1

The disciples saw Moses and Elijah standing next to Jesus.

3

5

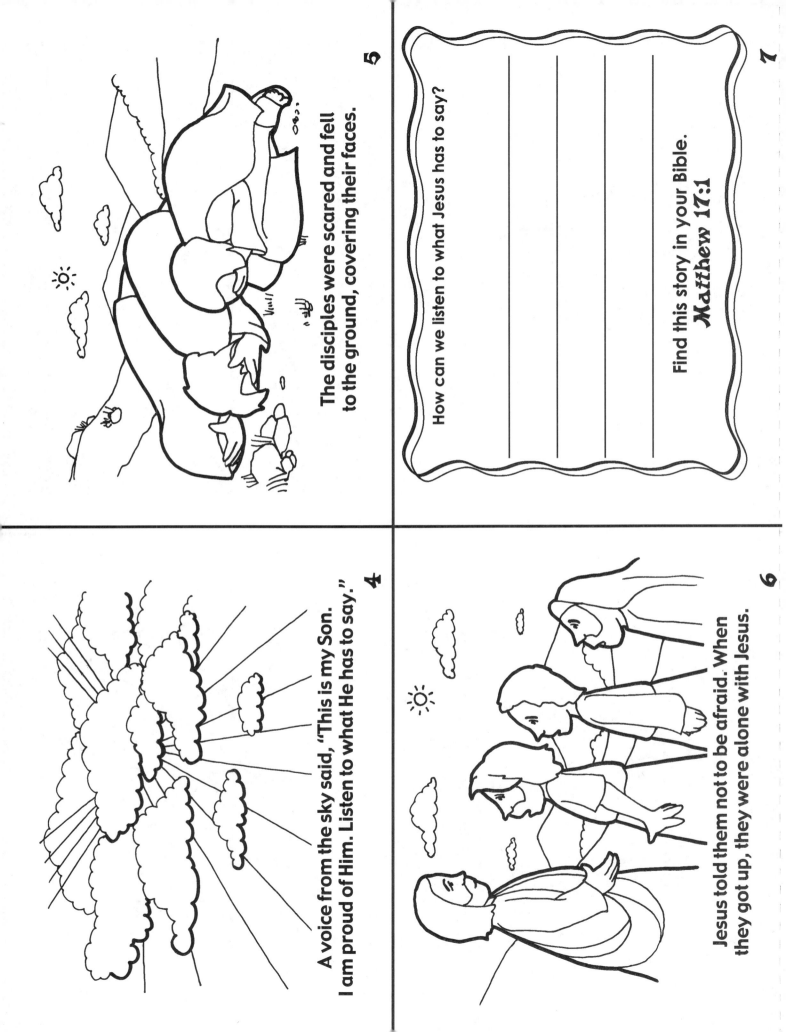

The disciples were scared and fell to the ground, covering their faces.

4

A voice from the sky said, "This is my Son. I am proud of Him. Listen to what He has to say."

7

How can we listen to what Jesus has to say?

Find this story in your Bible. *Matthew 17:1*

6

Jesus told them not to be afraid. When they got up, they were alone with Jesus.

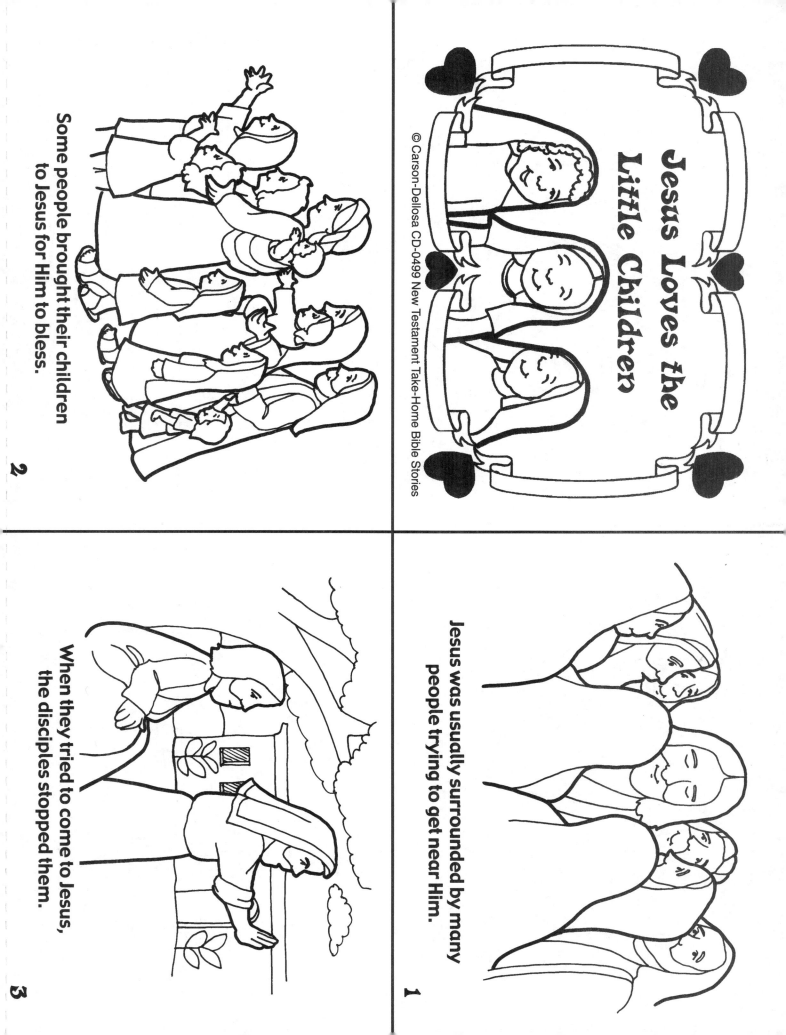

Jesus Loves the Little Children

Some people brought their children to Jesus for Him to bless.

2

Jesus was usually surrounded by many people trying to get near Him.

1

When they tried to come to Jesus, the disciples stopped them.

3

But Jesus said, "Let the children come to me."

How do grown-ups need to be more like children?

Find this story in your Bible.
Matthew 19:13

The disciples said that Jesus did not have time for children and told them to go away.

Jesus explained that they should be more like children—full of love and trust in Him.

The Rich Man and Lazarus

© Carson-Dellosa CD-0499 New Testament Take-Home Bible Stories

He didn't pay attention to people like Lazarus, the beggar who sat outside his house.

2

There once was a rich man who loved money and things more than he loved God.

1

The rich man died and went to hell. Lazarus died and angels carried him to be near Abraham.

3

Page 61

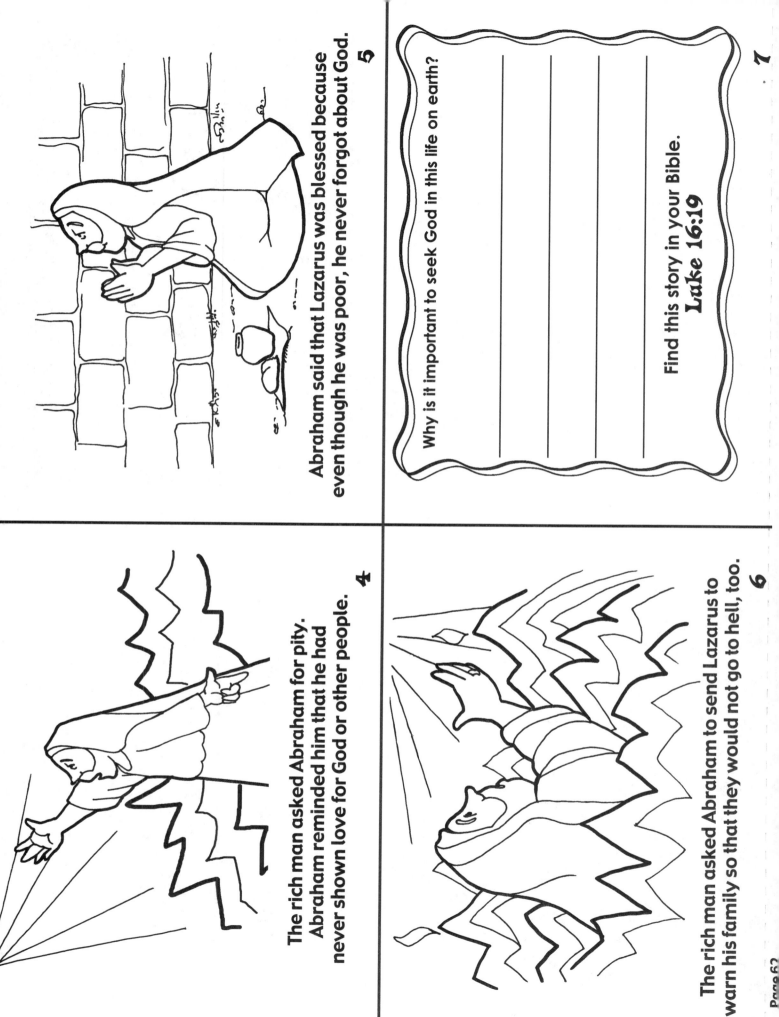

Abraham said that Lazarus was blessed because even though he was poor, he never forgot about God.

5

Why is it important to seek God in this life on earth?

_____

_____

_____

_____

Find this story in your Bible.
Luke 16:19

7

The rich man asked Abraham for pity. Abraham reminded him that he had never shown love for God or other people.

4

The rich man asked Abraham to send Lazarus to warn his family so that they would not go to hell, too.

6

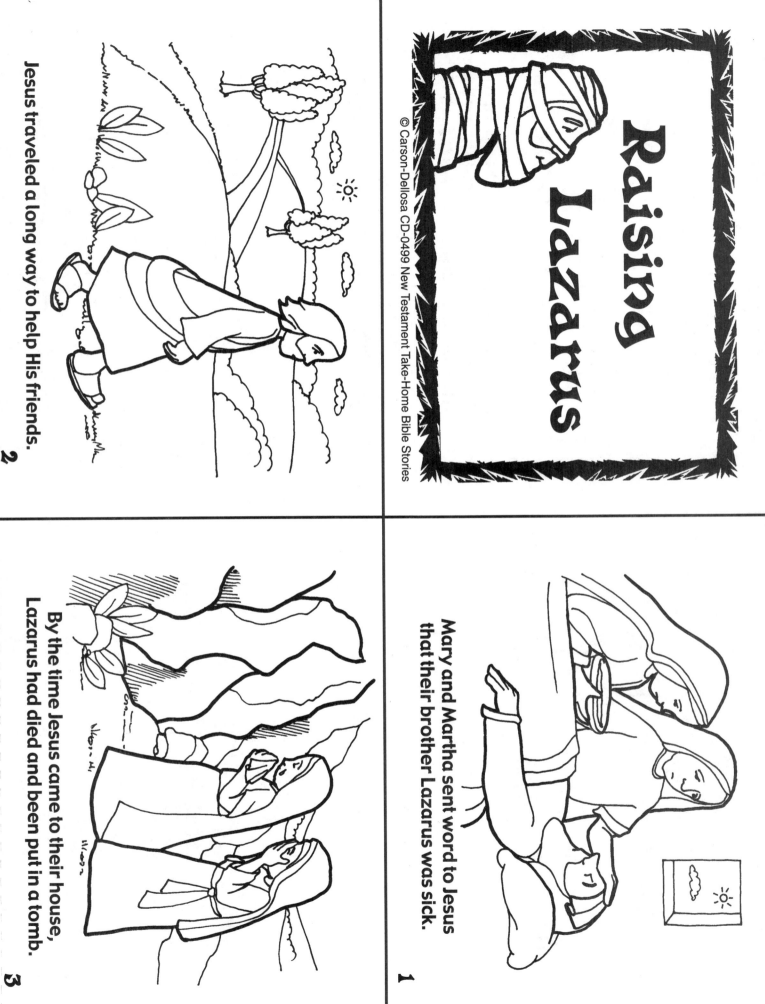

Raising Lazarus

Jesus traveled a long way to help His friends.

2

Mary and Martha sent word to Jesus that their brother Lazarus was sick.

1

By the time Jesus came to their house, Lazarus had died and been put in a tomb.

3

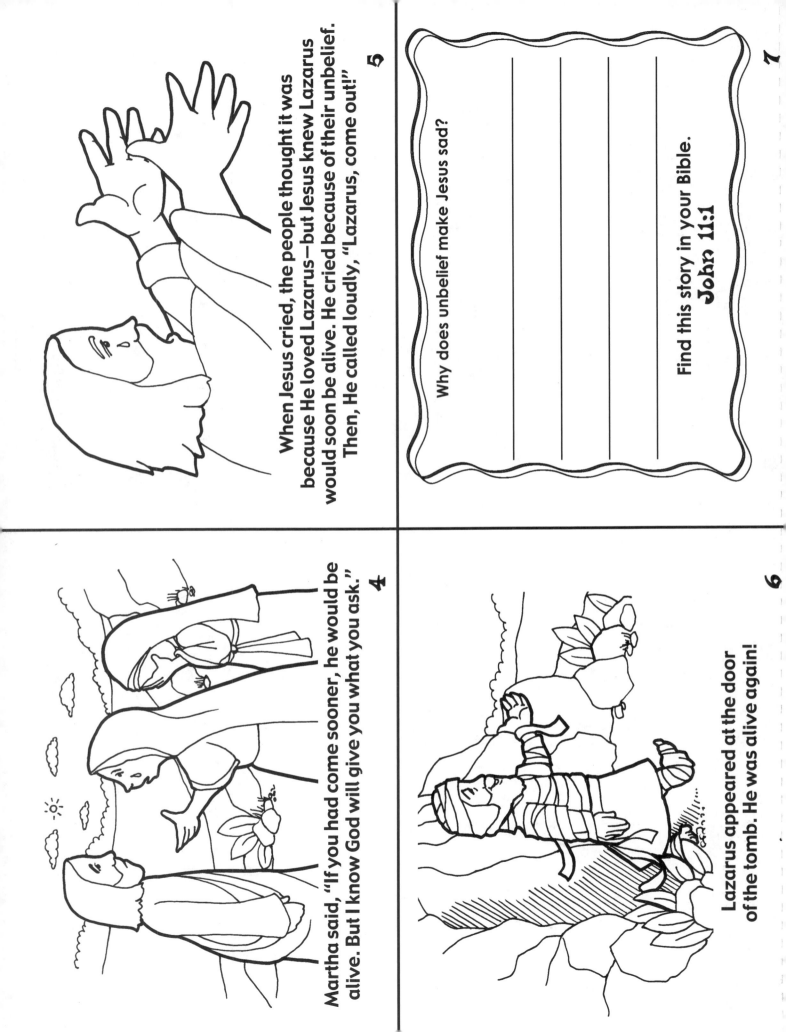

5

When Jesus cried, the people thought it was because He loved Lazarus—but Jesus knew Lazarus would soon be alive. He cried because of their unbelief. Then, He called loudly, "Lazarus, come out!"

7

Why does unbelief make Jesus sad?

Find this story in your Bible. **John 11:1**

4

Martha said, "If you had come sooner, he would be alive. But I know God will give you what you ask."

6

Lazarus appeared at the door of the tomb. He was alive again!

The Thankful Man

They had leprosy—a disease that made people stay far away from them.

2

Ten men came to Jesus looking for help.

1

From a long way away they shouted, "Please help us!"

3

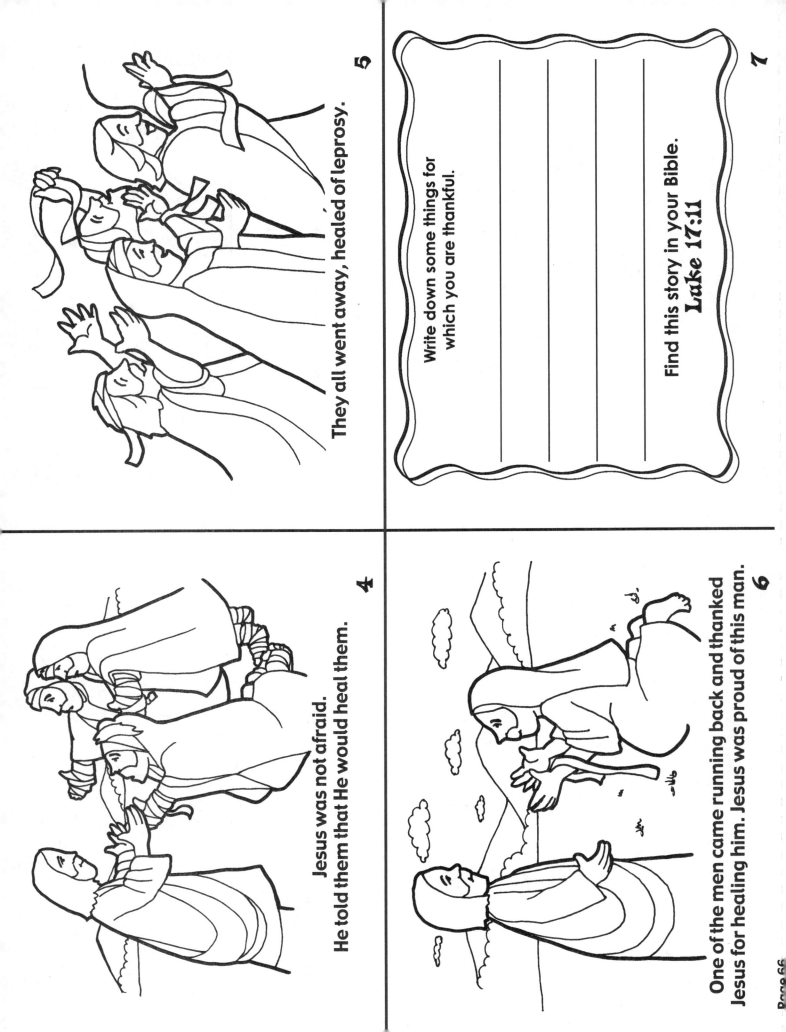

5

They all went away, healed of leprosy.

7

Write down some things for which you are thankful.

Find this story in your Bible.
Luke 17:11

4

Jesus was not afraid.
He told them that He would heal them.

6

One of the men came running back and thanked Jesus for healing him. Jesus was proud of this man.

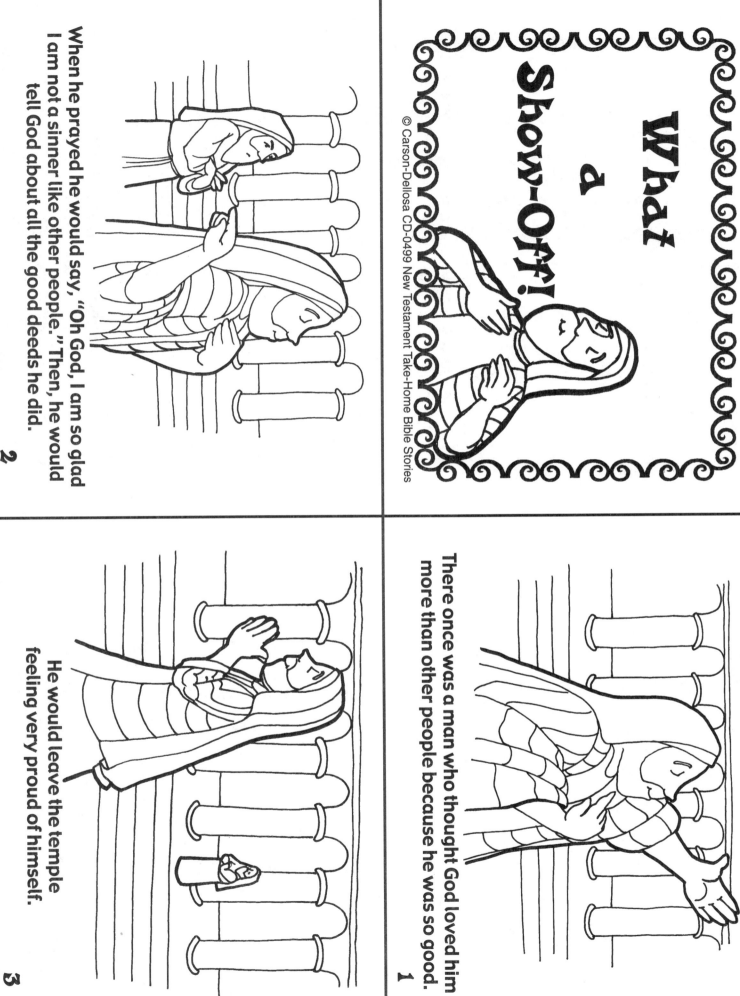

What a Show-Off!

When he prayed he would say, "Oh God, I am so glad I am not a sinner like other people." Then, he would tell God about all the good deeds he did.

2

There once was a man who thought God loved him more than other people because he was so good.

1

He would leave the temple feeling very proud of himself.

3

5

He would pray to God and say, "Lord, I'm sorry for all the bad things I've done."

7

Why should we be more like the man who was sorry?

_____

_____

_____

_____

_____

Find this story in your Bible.
Luke 18:9

4

There was another man who came to the temple looking very sad.

6

Jesus said that the man who was sorry pleased God because he did not brag about being good.

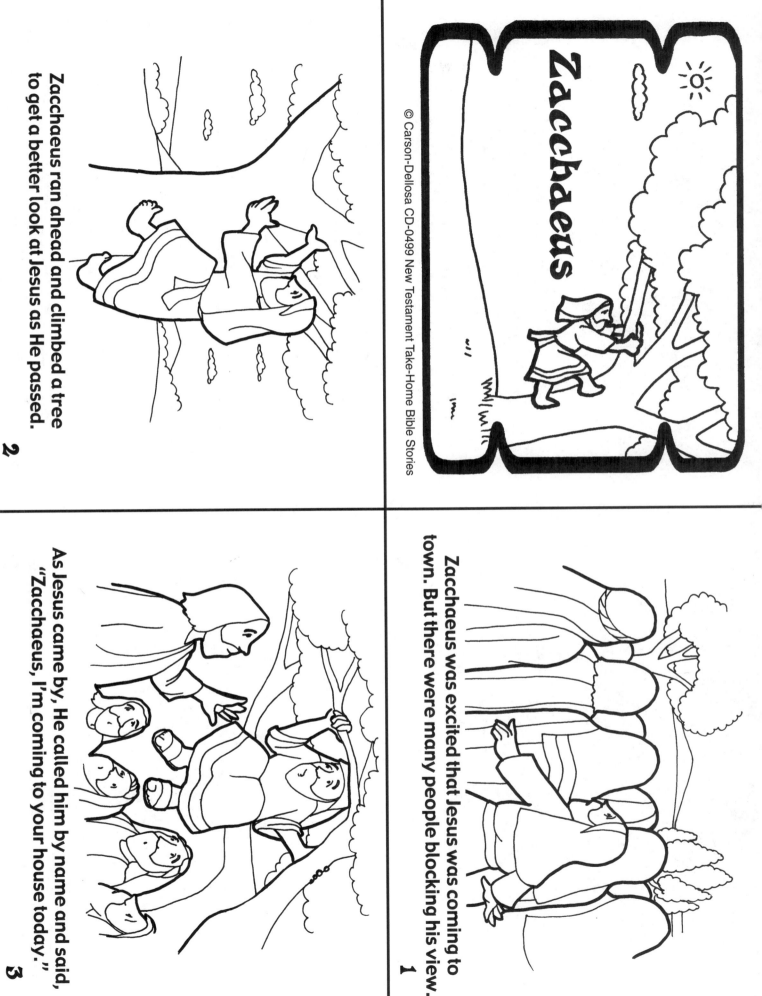

Zaccaeus ran ahead and climbed a tree to get a better look at Jesus as He passed.

2

Zacchaeus

Zacchaeus was excited that Jesus was coming to town. But there were many people blocking his view.

1

As Jesus came by, He called him by name and said, "Zacchaeus, I'm coming to your house today."

3

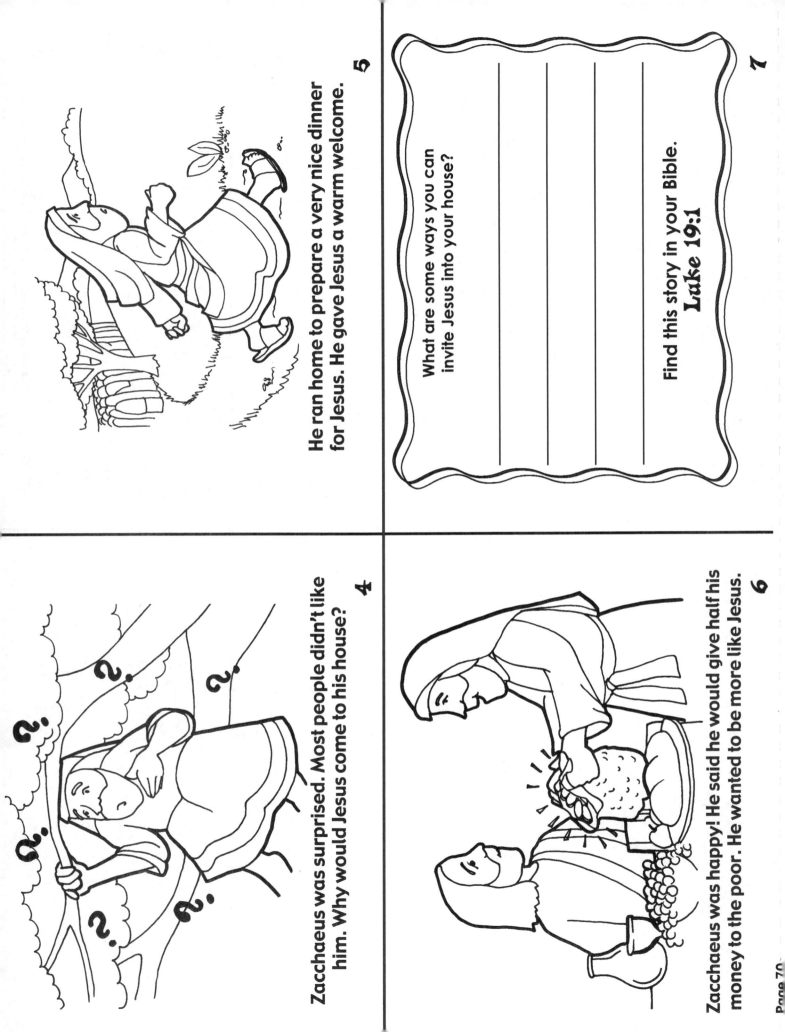

He ran home to prepare a very nice dinner for Jesus. He gave Jesus a warm welcome.

5

What are some ways you can invite Jesus into your house?

Find this story in your Bible.
Luke 19:1

7

Zacchaeus was surprised. Most people didn't like him. Why would Jesus come to his house?

4

Zacchaeus was happy! He said he would give half his money to the poor. He wanted to be more like Jesus.

6

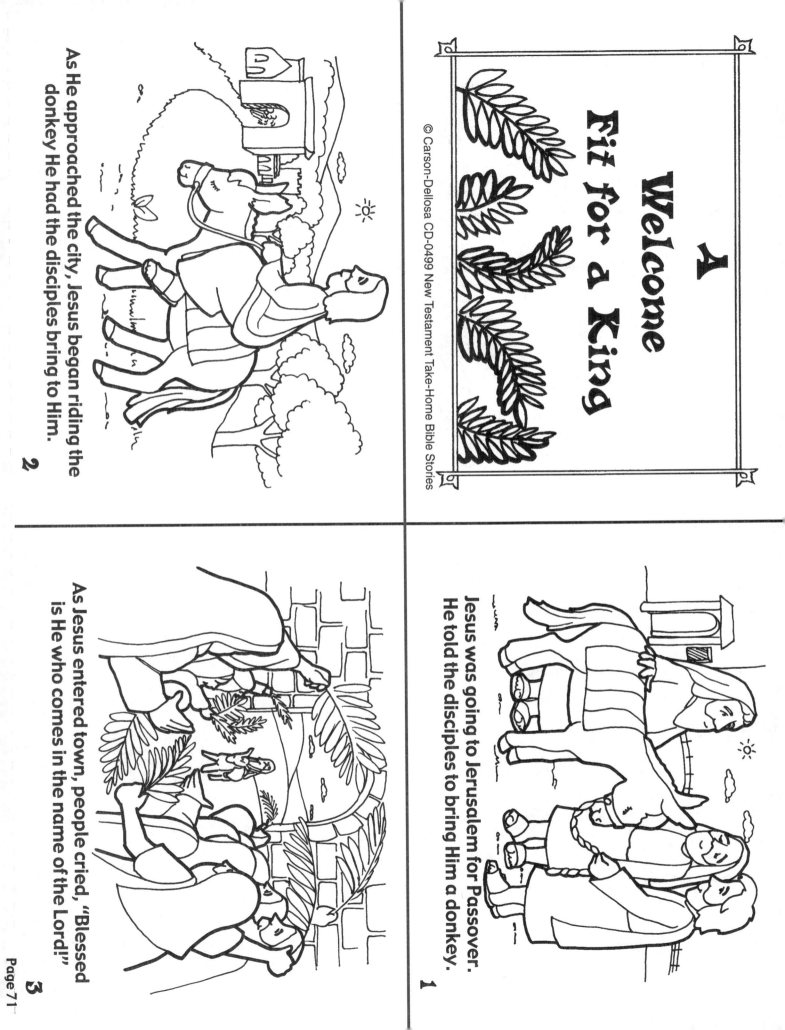

Welcome

Fit for a King

As He approached the city, Jesus began riding the donkey He had the disciples bring to Him.

2

Jesus was going to Jerusalem for Passover. He told the disciples to bring Him a donkey.

1

As Jesus entered town, people cried, "Blessed is He who comes in the name of the Lord!"

3

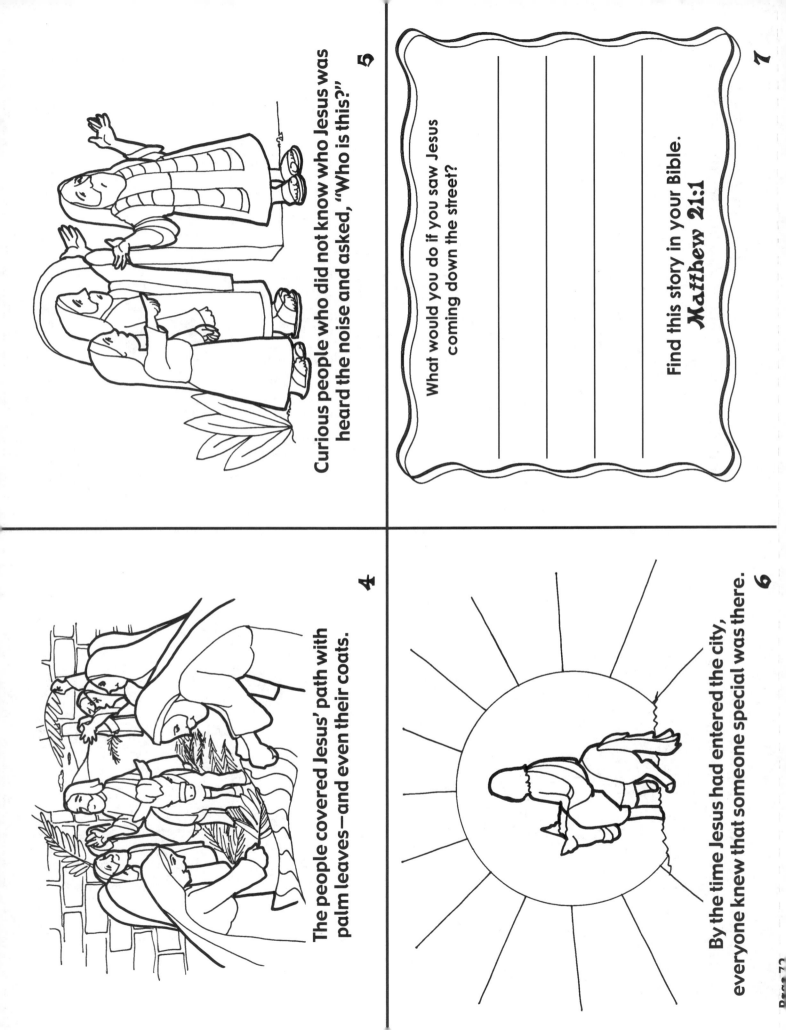

5

Curious people who did not know who Jesus was heard the noise and asked, "Who is this?"

7

What would you do if you saw Jesus coming down the street?

_____

_____

_____

_____

Find this story in your Bible.
Matthew 21:1

4

The people covered Jesus' path with palm leaves—and even their coats.

6

By the time Jesus had entered the city, everyone knew that someone special was there.

The Greatest Commandment

© Carson-Dellosa CD-0499 New Testament Take-Home Bible Stories

They asked Jesus, "What is the greatest commandment?"

2

Some people tried to trick Jesus by asking Him what they thought were hard questions.

1

He said, "The greatest commandment is to love God."

Love God

3

5

Love One Another

But then Jesus said, "The second commandment is this: 'Love one another.'"

7

Name some ways we can show love to others.

_____

_____

_____

_____

Find this story in your Bible.
Matthew 22:34

4

This means we should worship God and pray. We should read His Word and do what He says.

6

I Love You! God

This means we are to love the people around us, just like we love ourselves.

A
Woman Gives All She Has

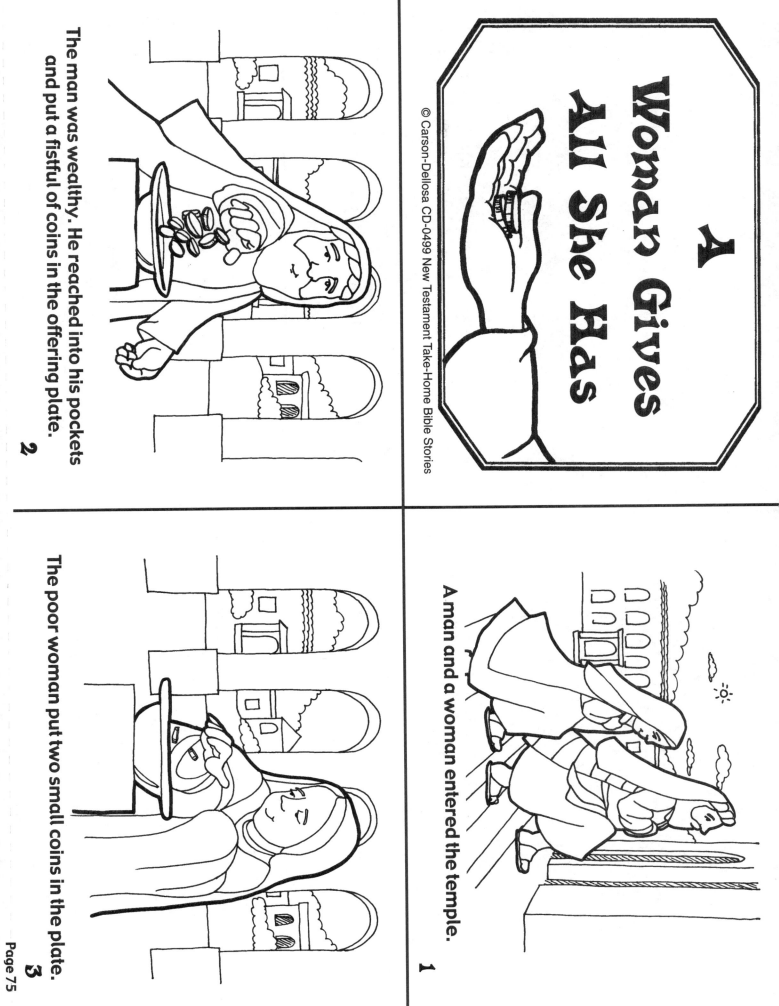

The man was wealthy. He reached into his pockets and put a fistful of coins in the offering plate.

2

A man and a woman entered the temple.

1

The poor woman put two small coins in the plate.

3

5

The people said, "The man, because he gave a lot of money."

7

Write some of the things that God provides for you.

Find this story in your Bible.
Luke 21:1

4

Jesus asked the people,
"Who gave the biggest offering?"

6

Jesus said that the woman actually gave the most because she gave all that she had. She trusted God to provide the things she needed.

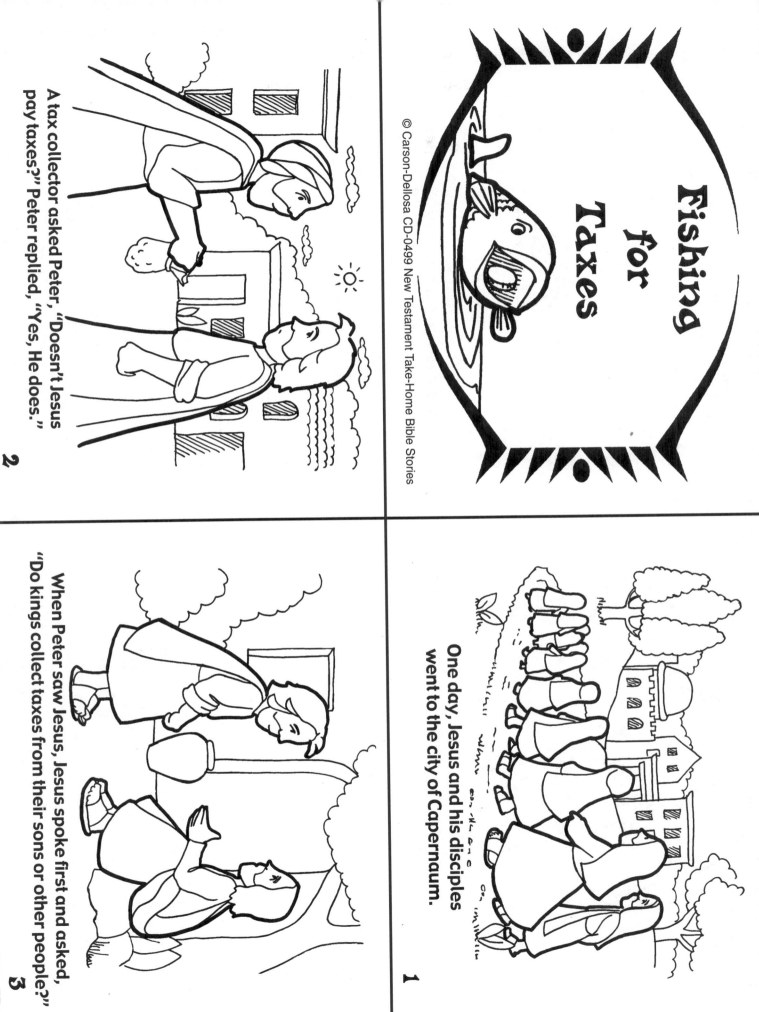

Fishing for Taxes

© Carson-Dellosa CD-0499 New Testament Take-Home Bible Stories

A tax collector asked Peter, "Doesn't Jesus pay taxes?" Peter replied, "Yes, He does."

2

One day, Jesus and his disciples went to the city of Capernaum.

1

When Peter saw Jesus, Jesus spoke first and asked, "Do kings collect taxes from their sons or other people?"

3

Jesus said, "Then, the sons are free. But go catch a fish and get our tax money out of its mouth."

5

How do you think Peter felt looking in a fish's mouth for money?

Find this story in your Bible.
Matthew 17:24

7

"From other people," Peter answered.

4

Peter did as Jesus said and paid both of their taxes.

6

Judas Betrays Jesus

Judas loved money. Sometimes he stole money from the treasury.

2

The religious leaders told Judas they would give him money if he agreed to give Jesus to them.

3

Judas was one of Jesus' disciples. He was in charge of the money Jesus used in His ministry.

1

5

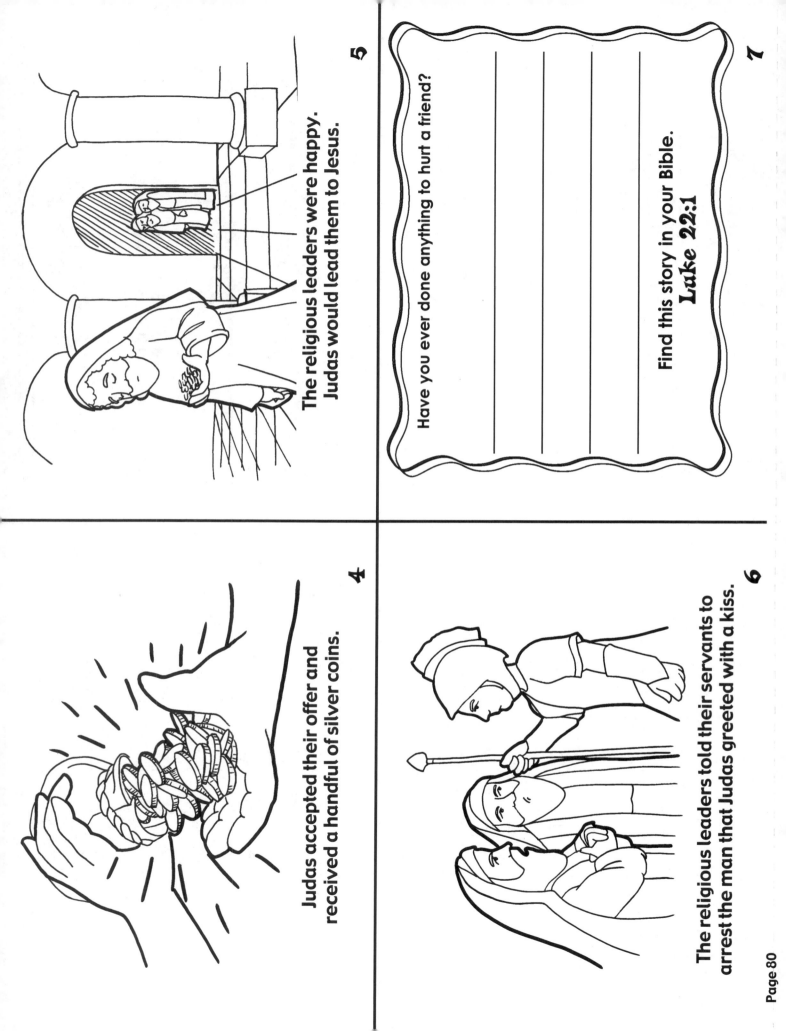

The religious leaders were happy.
Judas would lead them to Jesus.

7

Have you ever done anything to hurt a friend?

Find this story in your Bible.
Luke 22:1

4

Judas accepted their offer and
received a handful of silver coins.

6

The religious leaders told their servants to
arrest the man that Judas greeted with a kiss.

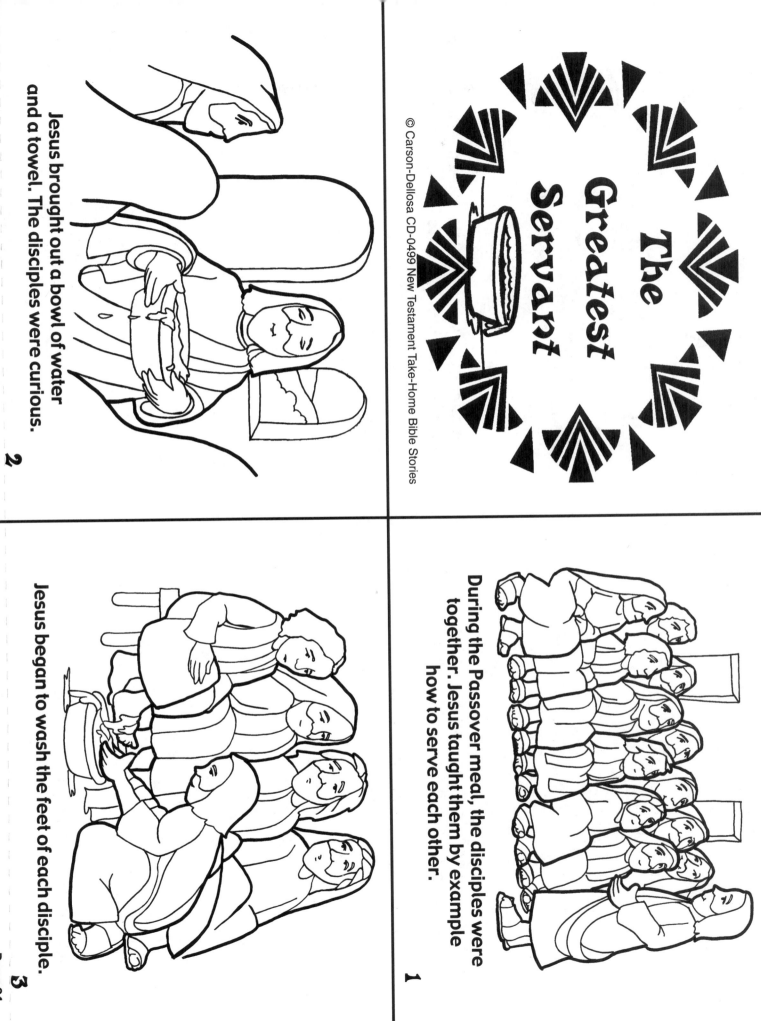

Jesus brought out a bowl of water and a towel. The disciples were curious.

2

The Greatest Servant

During the Passover meal, the disciples were together. Jesus taught them by example how to serve each other.

1

Jesus began to wash the feet of each disciple.

3

Jesus continued washing Peter's feet. Jesus told him that to be in His life, he had to let Him wash his feet.

5

What are some ways you can serve other people like Jesus did?

_____

_____

_____

_____

Find this story in your Bible.
John 13:1

7

When He got to Peter, Peter pulled his feet away. "I'm not good enough for you to wash my feet!"

4

Peter jumped up and said, "Wash my hands and my head, too!" Jesus said, "To wash your feet is enough."

6

The Last Supper

He explained to the disciples what would happen in the next few days.

2

Jesus celebrated the Passover with His disciples. He knew this would be His last meal before He died.

1

Jesus said that Judas would betray Him and Peter would deny Him. The disciples couldn't believe their ears!

3

He took a cup of wine and said, "This is my blood that I give for you. When you drink it, remember me."

5

What does the bread and the wine of the Passover meal represent?

_____
_____
_____
_____
_____

Find this story in your Bible. *Matthew 26:17*

7

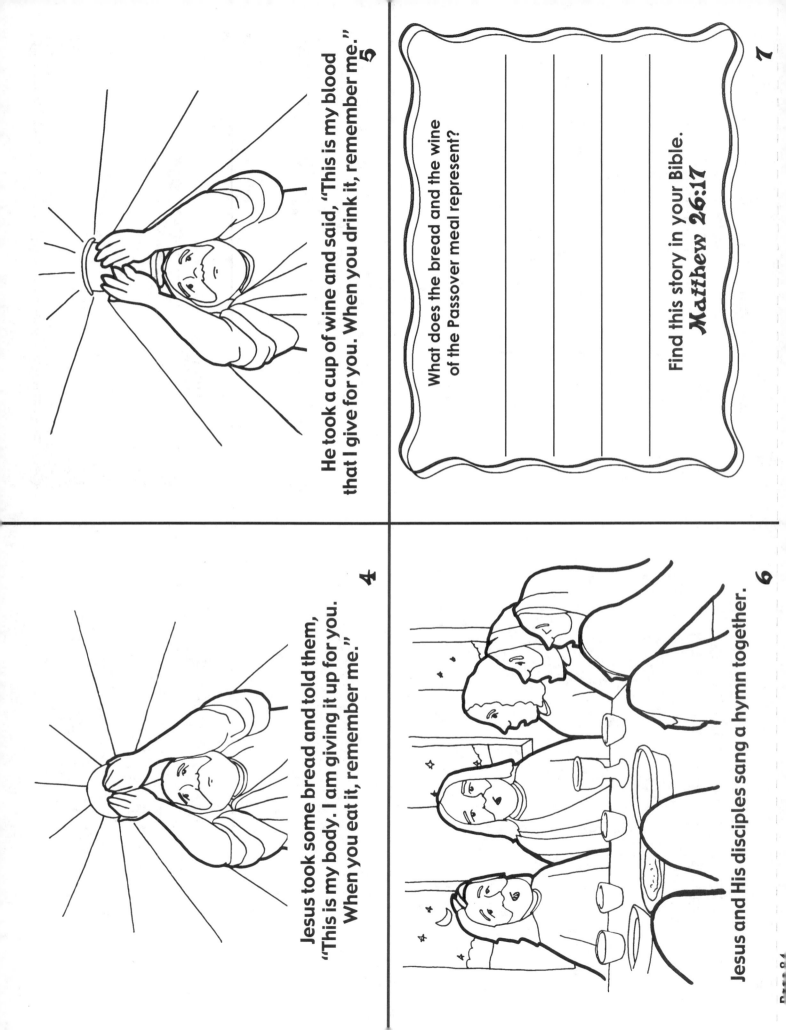

Jesus took some bread and told them, "This is my body. I am giving it up for you. When you eat it, remember me."

4

Jesus and His disciples sang a hymn together.

6

So He went with some of the disciples to a garden.

2

Prayers in the Garden

He told the disciples, "Wait here for me."

3

Jesus knew it was almost time for Him to be crucified. He wanted to pray to God first.

1

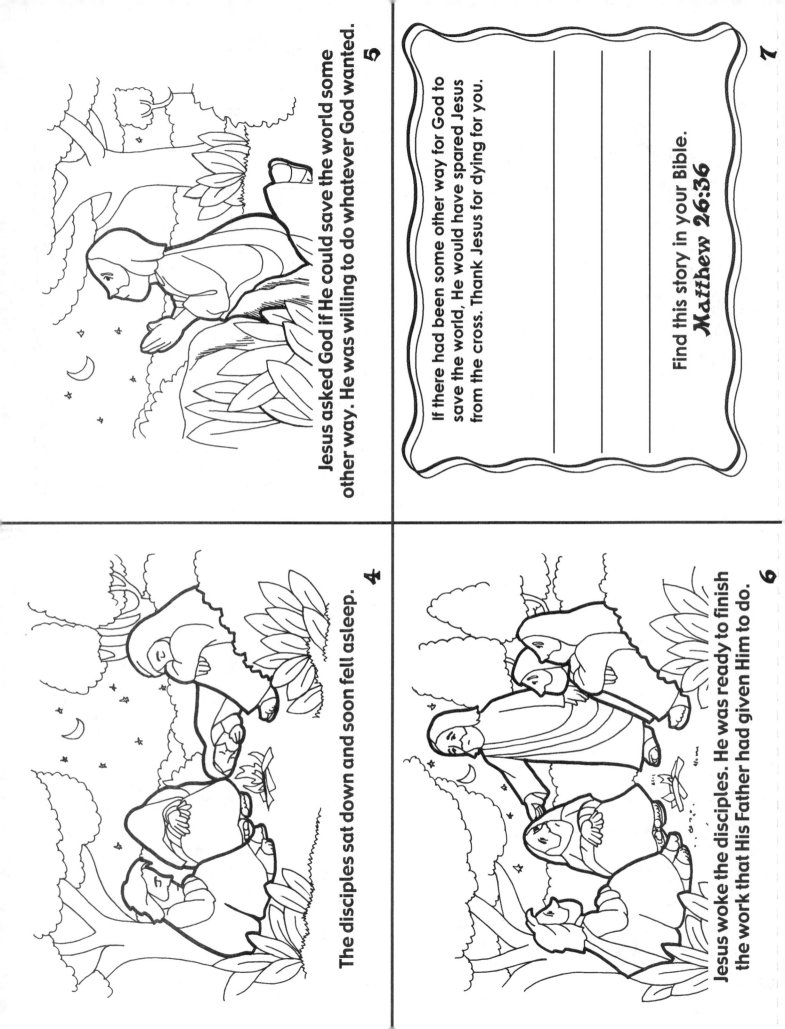

5

Jesus asked God if He could save the world some other way. He was willing to do whatever God wanted.

7

If there had been some other way for God to save the world, He would have spared Jesus from the cross. Thank Jesus for dying for you.

Find this story in your Bible.
Matthew 26:36

4

The disciples sat down and soon fell asleep.

6

Jesus woke the disciples. He was ready to finish the work that His Father had given Him to do.

Judas was leading them to Jesus. He kissed Jesus as a sign to the men that He was the one to arrest.

2

The Arrest

Jesus said, "Judas, do you betray me with a kiss?"

3

While Jesus and His disciples were in the garden, they heard a group of people approaching.

1

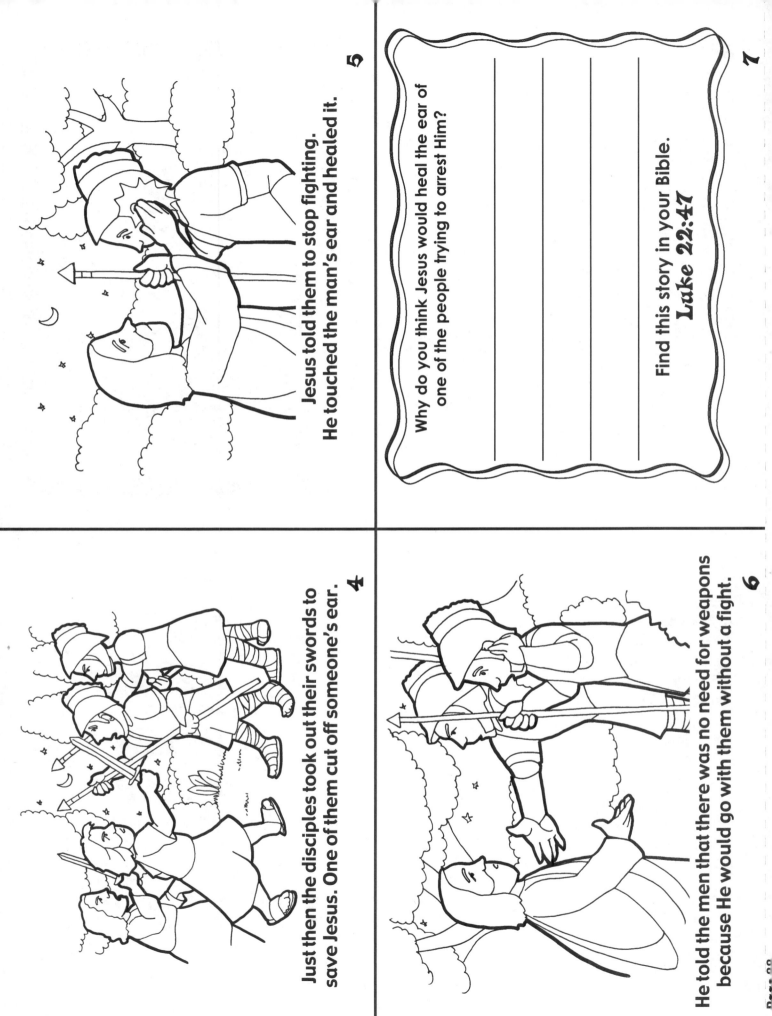

Jesus told them to stop fighting.
He touched the man's ear and healed it.

Why do you think Jesus would heal the ear of
one of the people trying to arrest Him?

Find this story in your Bible.
Luke 22:47

Just then the disciples took out their swords to
save Jesus. One of them cut off someone's ear.

He told the men that there was no need for weapons
because He would go with them without a fight.

Peter Denies Jesus

© Carson-Dellosa CD-0499 New Testament Take-Home Bible Stories

He waited outside the building where Jesus had been taken.

2

A servant girl said, "I saw you with Jesus." But Peter said, "I don't know what you're talking about."

3

Peter was afraid that he would be arrested for being friends with Jesus.

1

Peter answered, "I don't know the man!"

Why did Peter lie about knowing Jesus?

Find this story in your Bible.
Matthew 26:69

Another girl said, "I'm sure it was you!"
Still others said, "We saw you, too."

Just then a rooster crowed—just as Jesus said.
Peter felt bad for what he had done and cried.

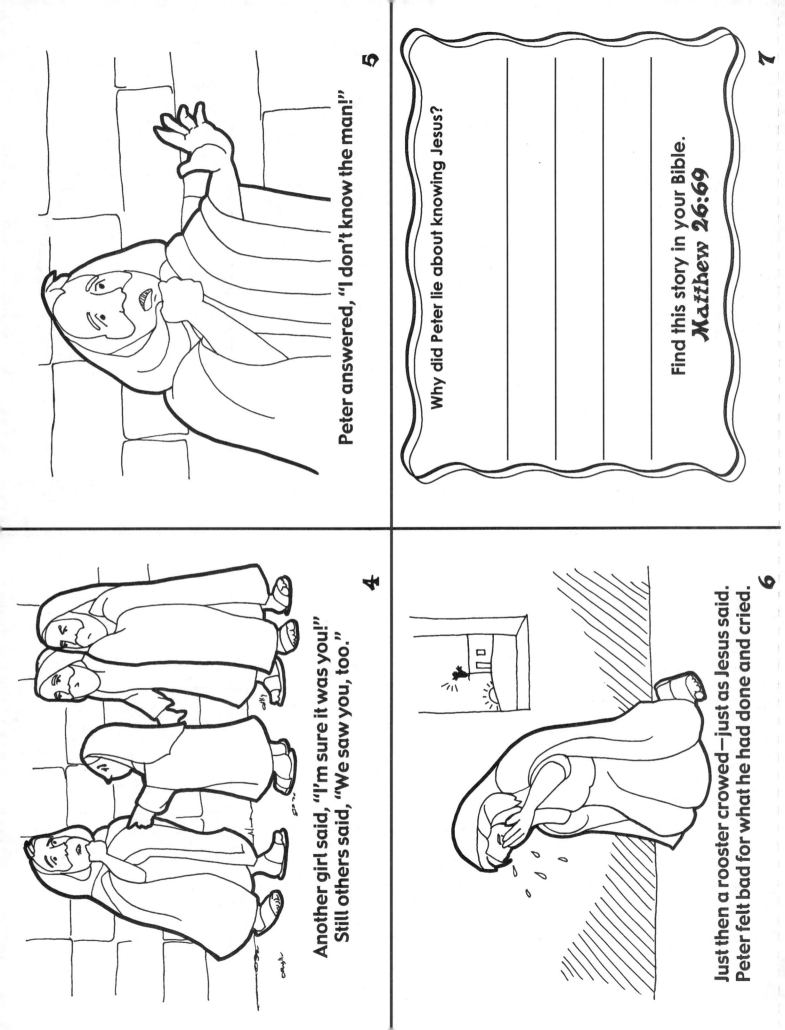

Pilate, a Roman governor, didn't think Jesus was dangerous. Pilate had Jesus taken to Herod.

2

Jesus' Trial

Jesus was arrested by temple guards and taken to the chief priests. They said Jesus was dangerous and should be taken before a Roman court.

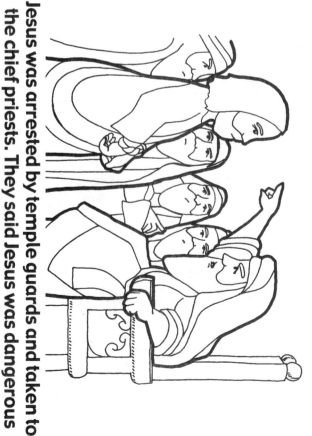

1

Jesus didn't answer any of Herod's questions. Herod made fun of Him and sent Him back to Pilate.

3

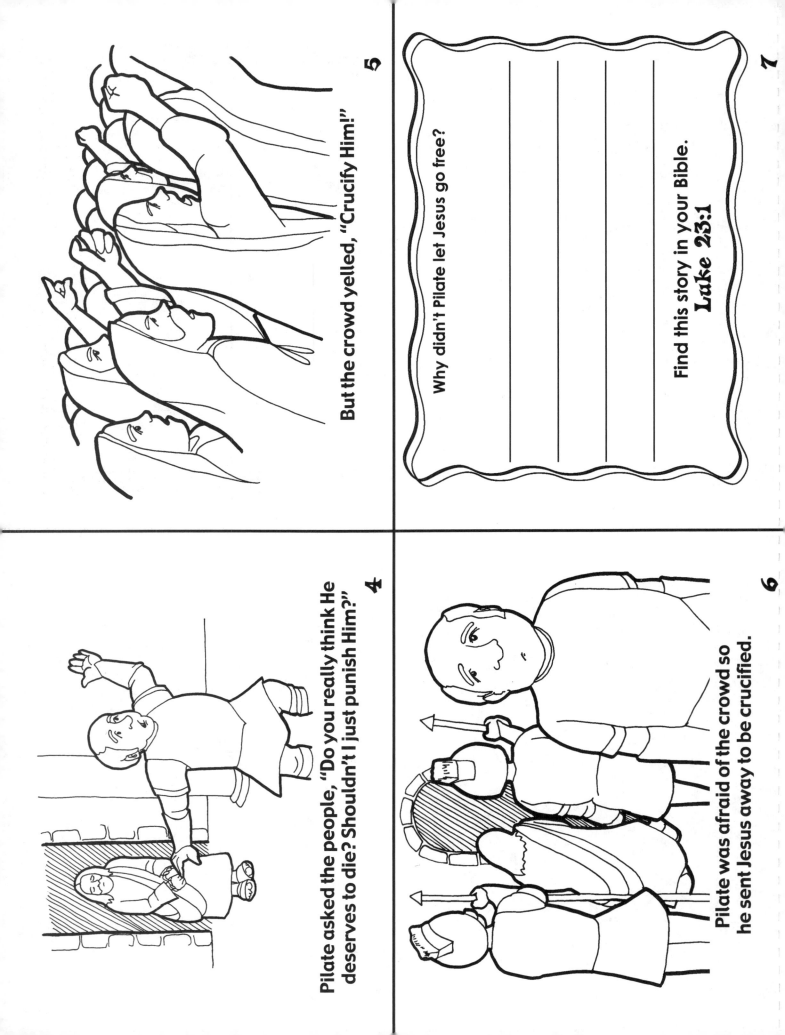

But the crowd yelled, "Crucify Him!"

5

Why didn't Pilate let Jesus go free?

Find this story in your Bible.
Luke 23:1

7

Pilate asked the people, "Do you really think He deserves to die? Shouldn't I just punish Him?"

4

Pilate was afraid of the crowd so he sent Jesus away to be crucified.

6

Crucifixion

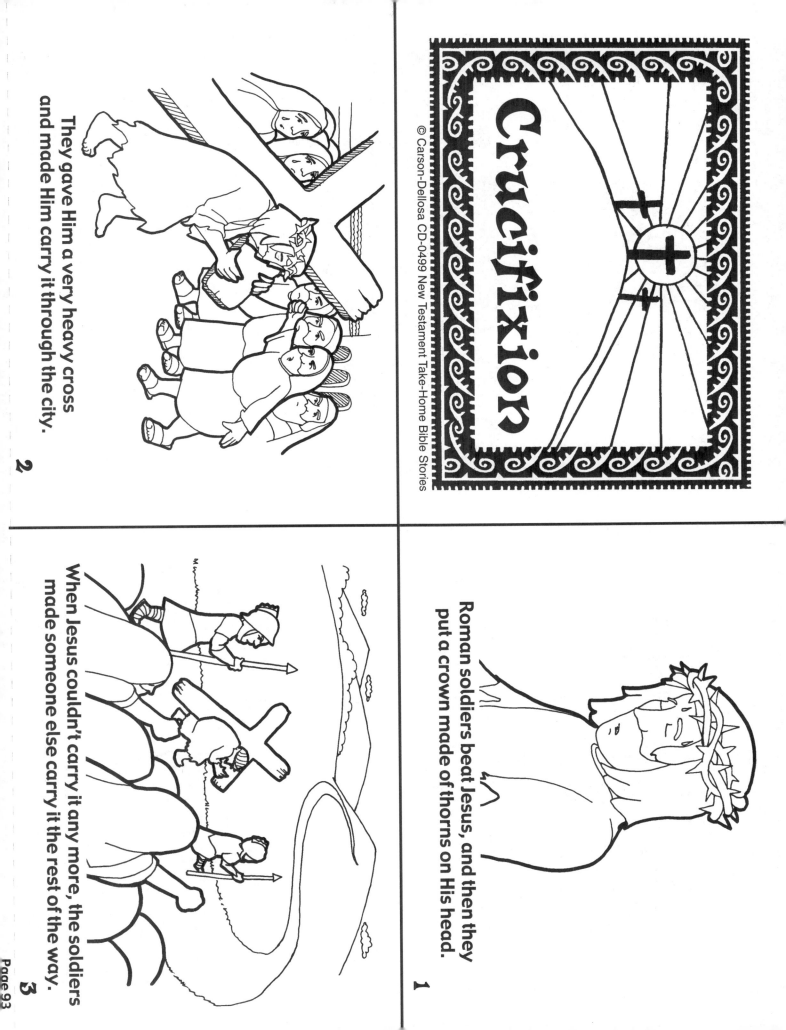

They gave Him a very heavy cross and made Him carry it through the city.

2

Roman soldiers beat Jesus, and then they put a crown made of thorns on His head.

1

When Jesus couldn't carry it any more, the soldiers made someone else carry it the rest of the way.

3

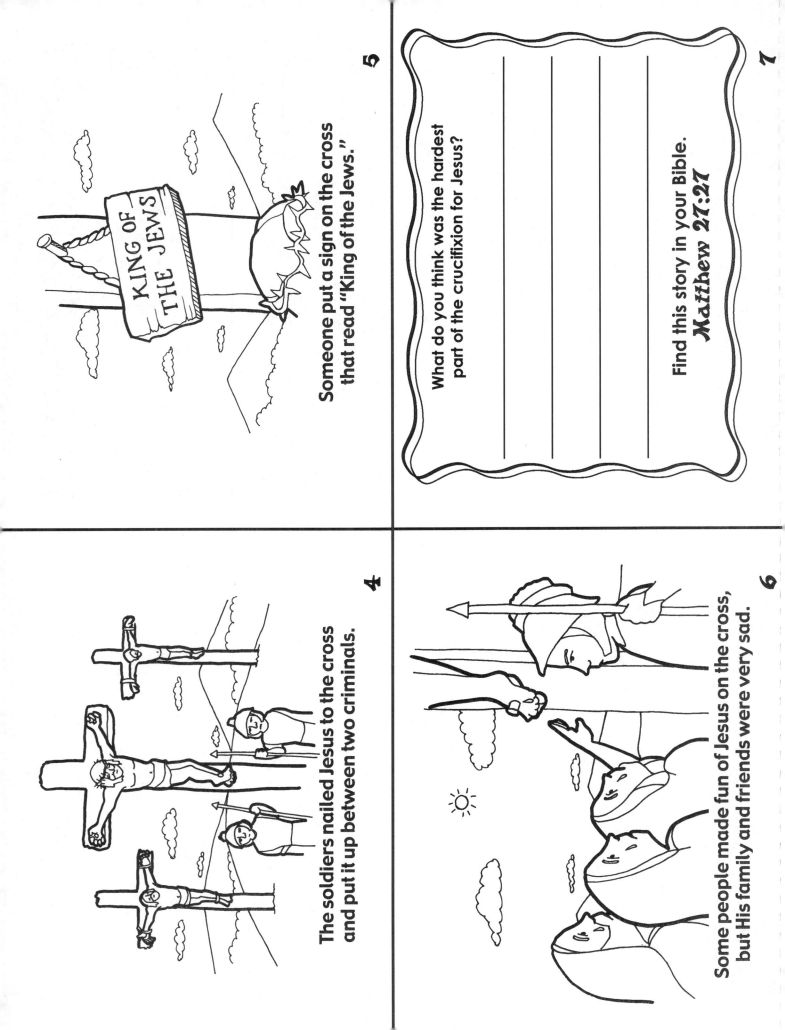

5

Someone put a sign on the cross that read "King of the Jews."

7

What do you think was the hardest part of the crucifixion for Jesus?

Find this story in your Bible. *Matthew 27:27*

4

The soldiers nailed Jesus to the cross and put it up between two criminals.

6

Some people made fun of Jesus on the cross, but His family and friends were very sad.

The Thief on the Cross

Both men had been caught doing bad things and were sentenced to be crucified.

2

Jesus was crucified between two thieves.

1

One of them told Jesus, "If you are who you say you are, save yourself and us!"

3

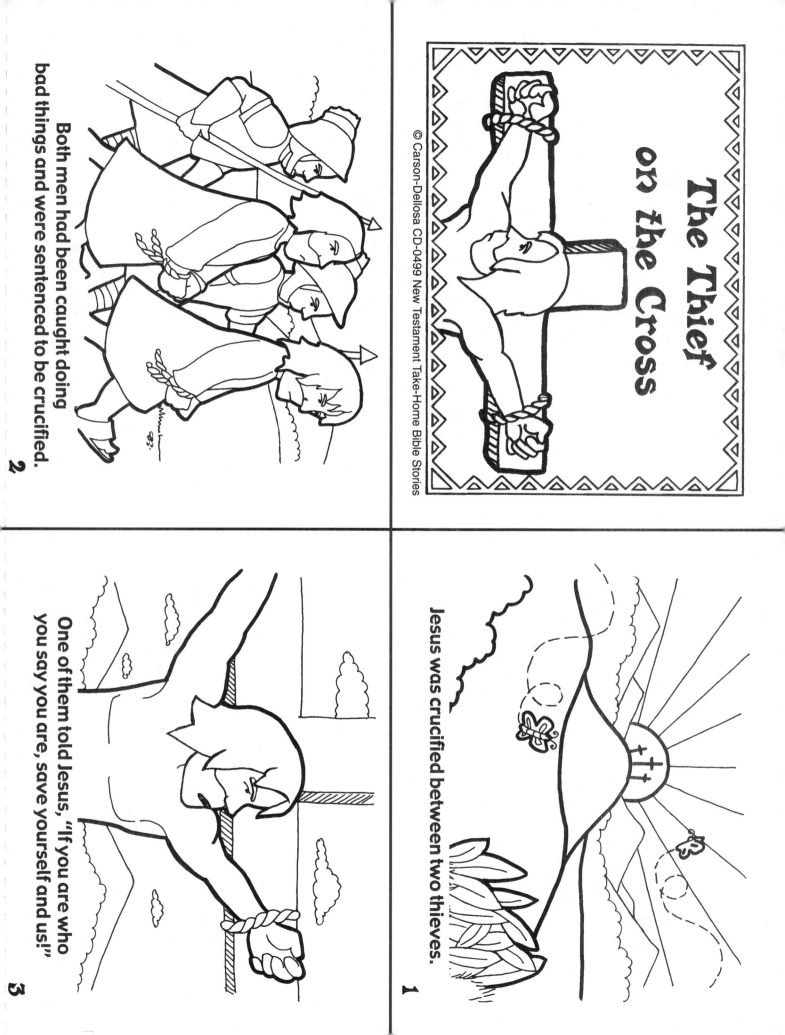

5

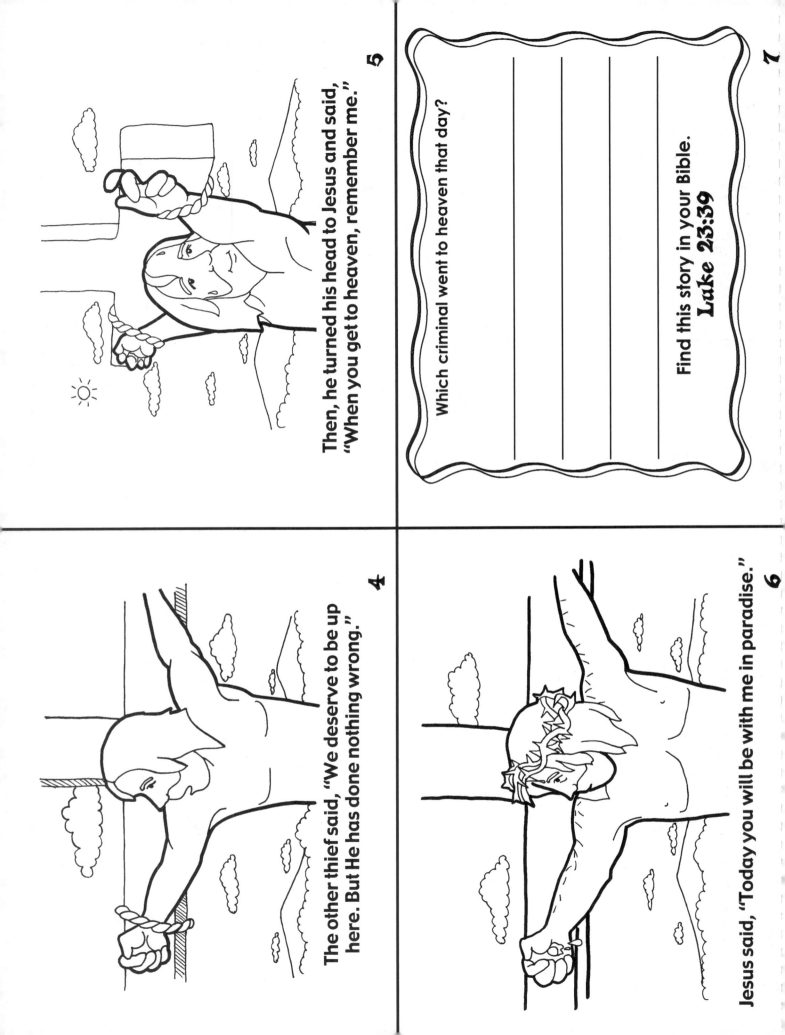

Then, he turned his head to Jesus and said,
"When you get to heaven, remember me."

7

Which criminal went to heaven that day?

_____

_____

_____

_____

Find this story in your Bible.
Luke 23:39

4

The other thief said, "We deserve to be up
here. But He has done nothing wrong."

6

Jesus said, "Today you will be with me in paradise."

When He was thirsty, the soldiers gave Him vinegar. He told His disciple John to care for His mother.

2

Jesus' Death

The sky turned black, and people were afraid.

3

Jesus hung on the cross for nine hours.

1

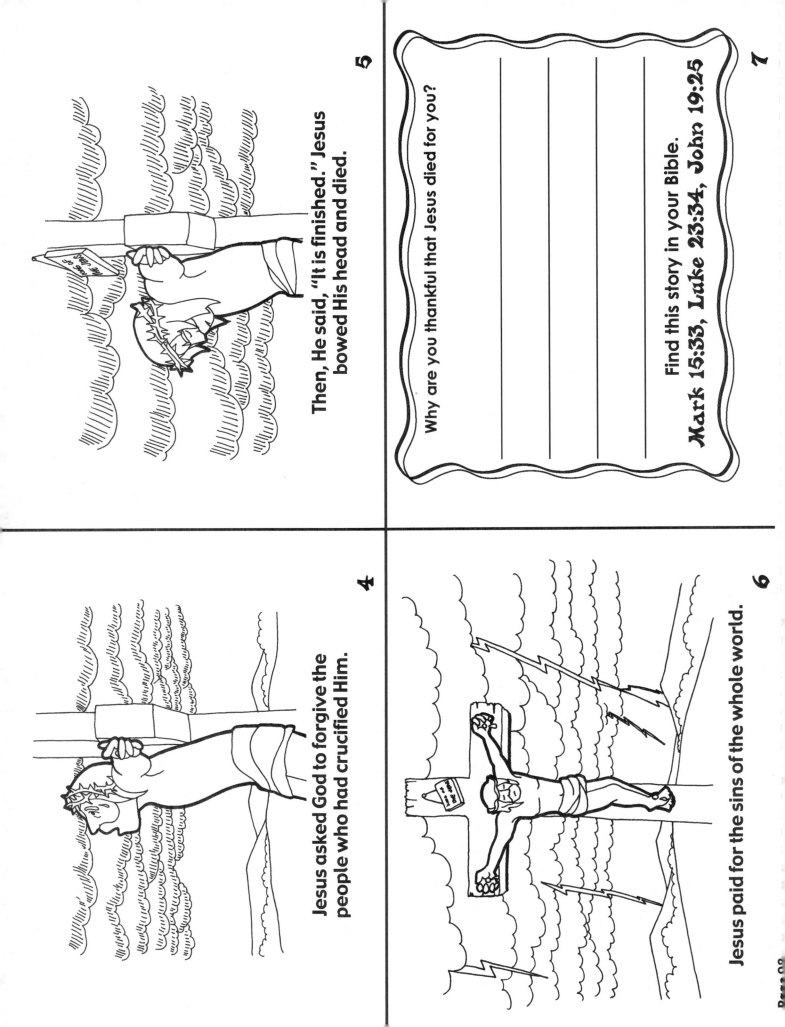

Then, He said, "It is finished." Jesus bowed His head and died.

Why are you thankful that Jesus died for you?

Find this story in your Bible.
Mark 15:33, Luke 23:34, John 19:25

4

Jesus asked God to forgive the people who had crucified Him.

Jesus paid for the sins of the whole world.

Resurrection

Three days after Jesus died, some women came to the tomb. The stone cover had been moved.

2

Jesus' body had been put in a tomb with a heavy stone blocking the entrance. Men guarded it.

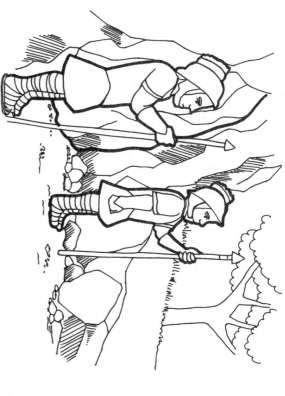

1

A man told them there was no one in the tomb. Mary asked where the body was. Then, she noticed the man she was talking to was Jesus. He was alive!

3

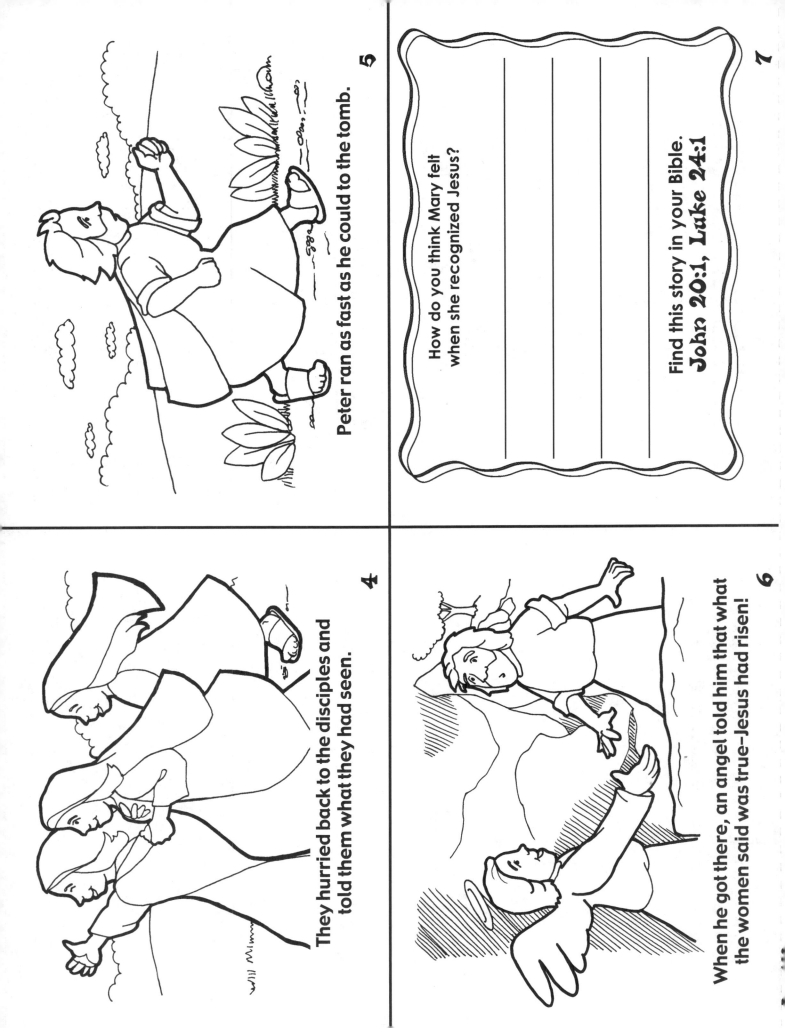

5

Peter ran as fast as he could to the tomb.

How do you think Mary felt when she recognized Jesus?

_____

_____

_____

_____

Find this story in your Bible.
John 20:1, Luke 24:1

They hurried back to the disciples and told them what they had seen.

When he got there, an angel told him that what the women said was true—Jesus had risen!

Doubting Thomas

1

The disciples were excited about the news that Jesus was alive. They gathered together and celebrated.

But Thomas did not believe. "Unless I see Him myself, I refuse to believe it."

2

A week later, the disciples were in a room with the doors locked. Suddenly, Jesus appeared!

3

5

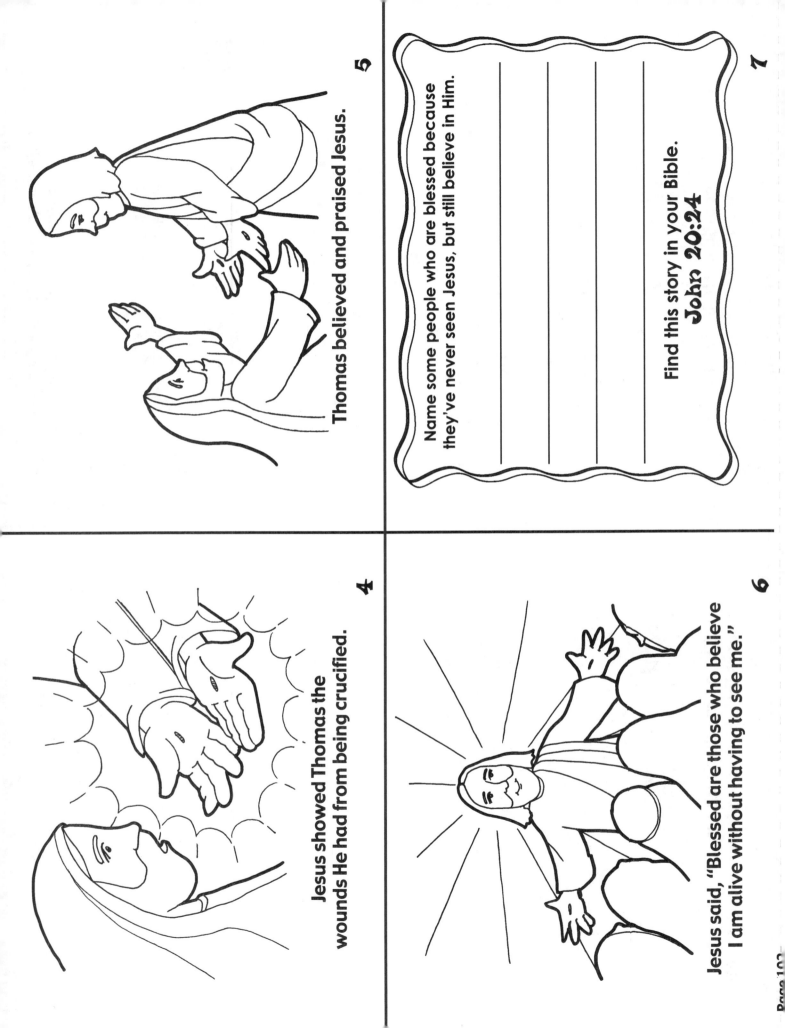

Thomas believed and praised Jesus.

7

Name some people who are blessed because they've never seen Jesus, but still believe in Him.

Find this story in your Bible.
John 20:24

4

Jesus showed Thomas the wounds He had from being crucified.

6

Jesus said, "Blessed are those who believe I am alive without having to see me."

Breakfast by the Sea

Jesus said, "Throw your net on the right side of the boat and you will."

2

After He had risen, Jesus called to His disciples as they fished, "Friends, haven't you caught any fish?"

1

The disciples did what Jesus said and caught so many fish that they couldn't lift the net.

3

The other disciples followed in the boat and came to shore. They found a fire burning and some fish and bread.

5

Why do you think Peter jumped in the water instead of waiting for the boat to get to shore?

_____

_____

_____

_____

Find this story in your Bible.
John 21:15

7

When Peter realized it was Jesus who had been speaking to them, he jumped in the water and swam to shore.

4

The disciples ate breakfast with Jesus.

6

Jesus Returns to Heaven

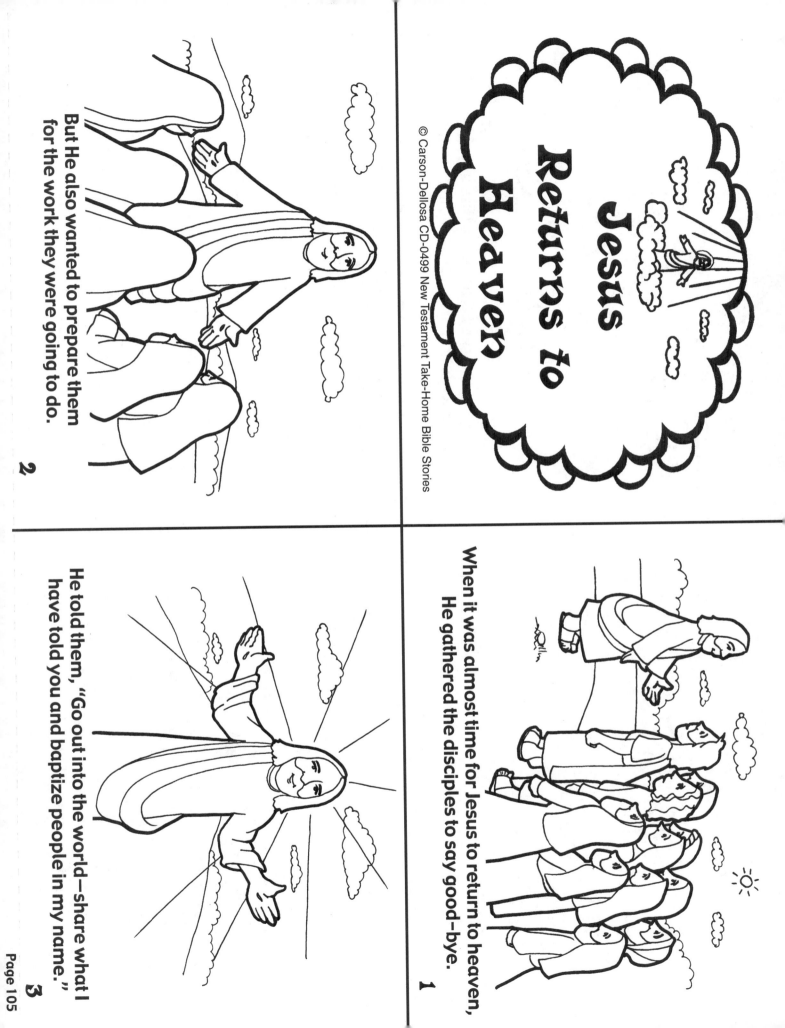

But He also wanted to prepare them for the work they were going to do.

2

When it was almost time for Jesus to return to heaven, He gathered the disciples to say good-bye.

1

He told them, "Go out into the world—share what I have told you and baptize people in my name."

3

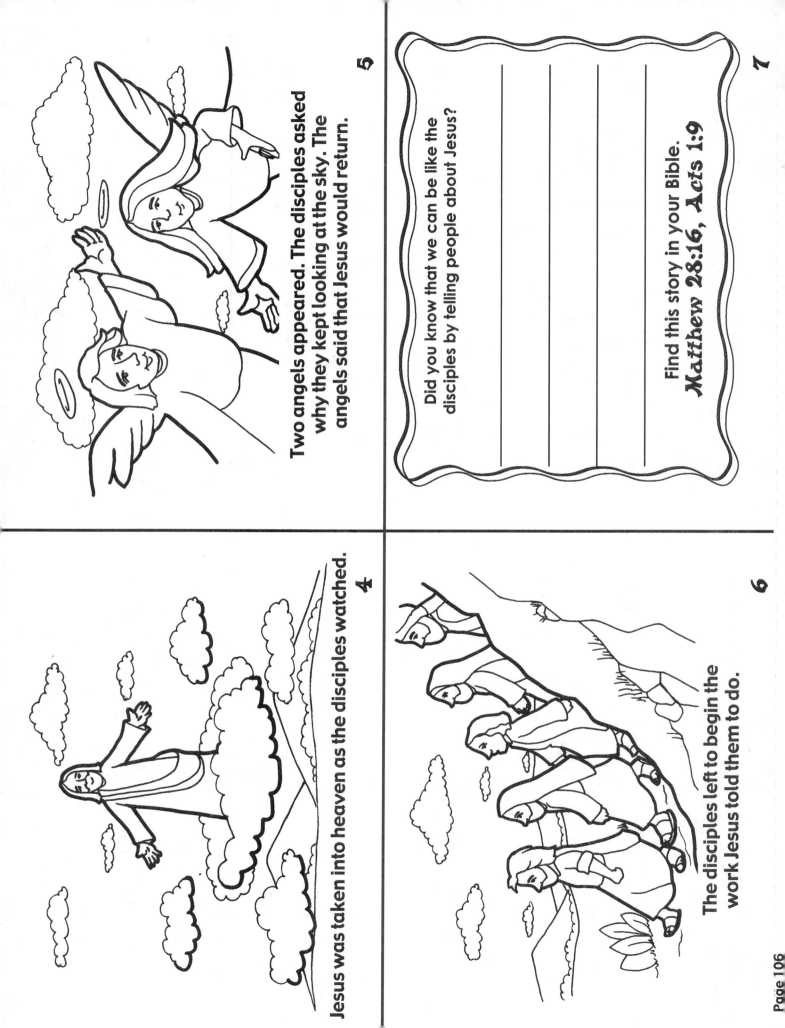

5

Two angels appeared. The disciples asked why they kept looking at the sky. The angels said that Jesus would return.

7

Did you know that we can be like the disciples by telling people about Jesus?

_____

_____

_____

_____

Find this story in your Bible.
Matthew 28:16, Acts 1:9

4

Jesus was taken into heaven as the disciples watched.

6

The disciples left to begin the work Jesus told them to do.

The Holy Spirit Comes

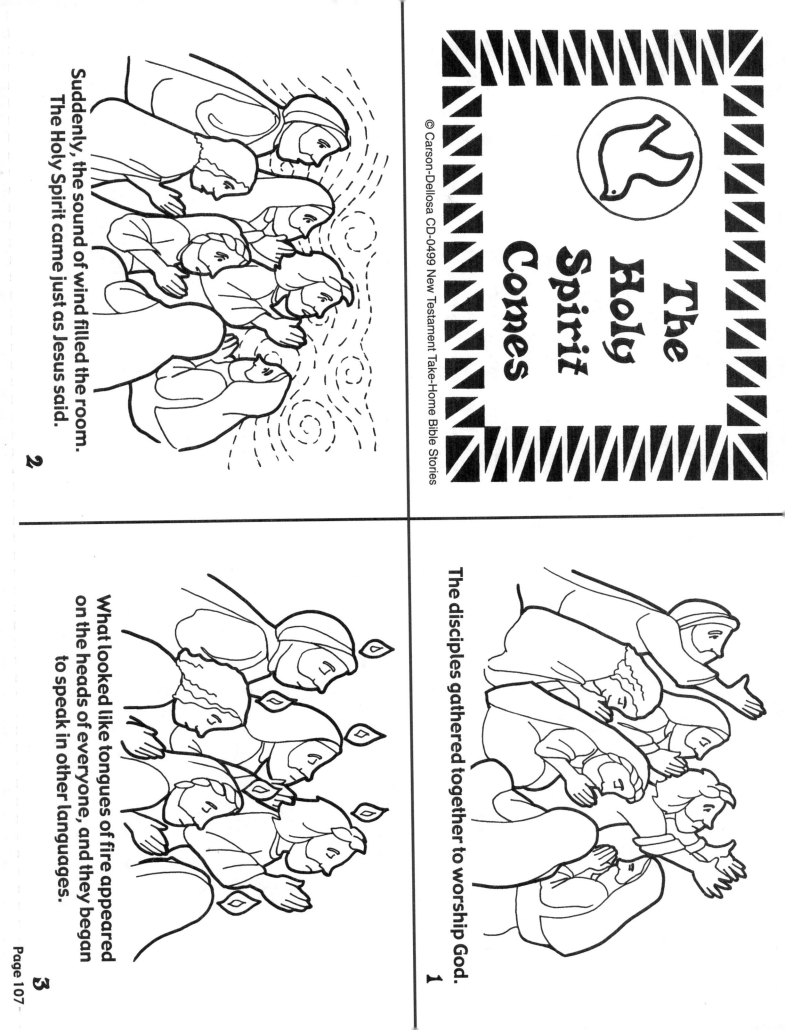

Suddenly, the sound of wind filled the room. The Holy Spirit came just as Jesus said.

2

The disciples gathered together to worship God.

1

What looked like tongues of fire appeared on the heads of everyone, and they began to speak in other languages.

3

5

Peter preached to them, "We are not drunk, we have received the gift of the Holy Spirit! This promise is for you and your children and for all whom the Lord calls."

7

Did you know that the same Holy Spirit is with us today?

Find this story in your Bible.
Acts 2:1

4

People walking by were shocked, saying, "Those people are drunk!"

6

About 3,000 people accepted Peter's message that day. The people praised God for saving them.

Peter and John on Trial

Temple guards arrested Peter and John and put them in jail overnight.

2

Religious leaders were upset because people were talking about Jesus rising from the dead.

1

The next day, Peter and John were on trial. They were asked who told them to preach about Jesus.

3

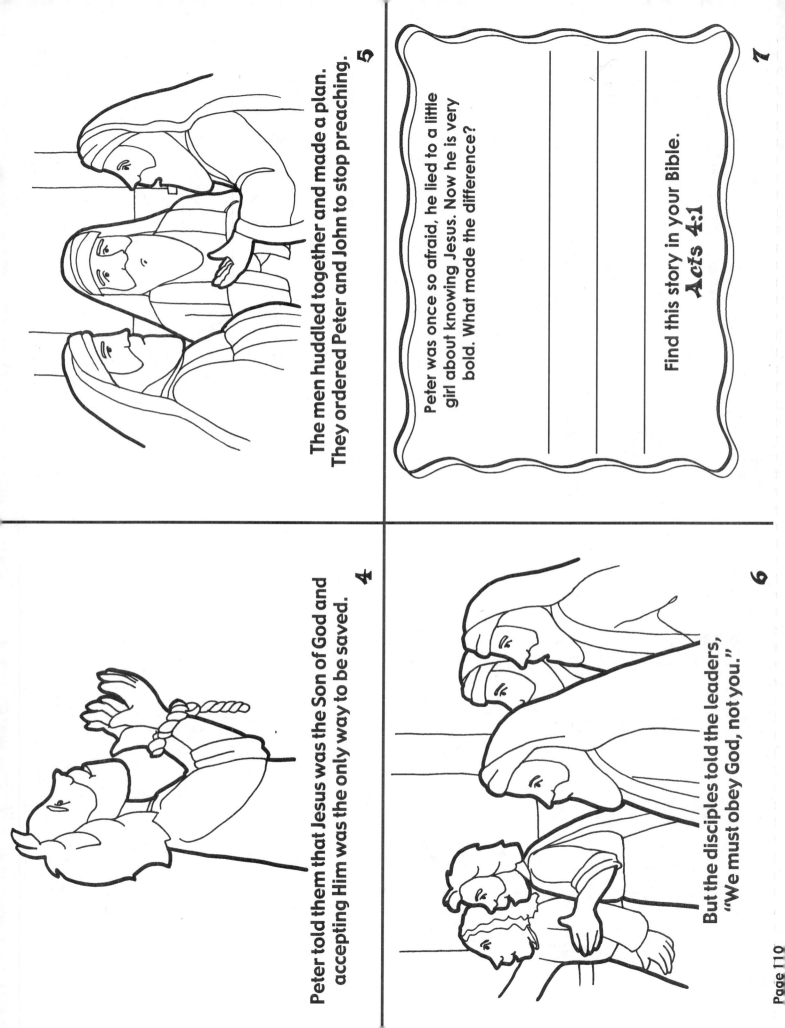

5

The men huddled together and made a plan. They ordered Peter and John to stop preaching.

7

Peter was once so afraid, he lied to a little girl about knowing Jesus. Now he is very bold. What made the difference?

Find this story in your Bible.
Acts 4:1

4

Peter told them that Jesus was the Son of God and accepting Him was the only way to be saved.

6

But the disciples told the leaders, "We must obey God, not you."

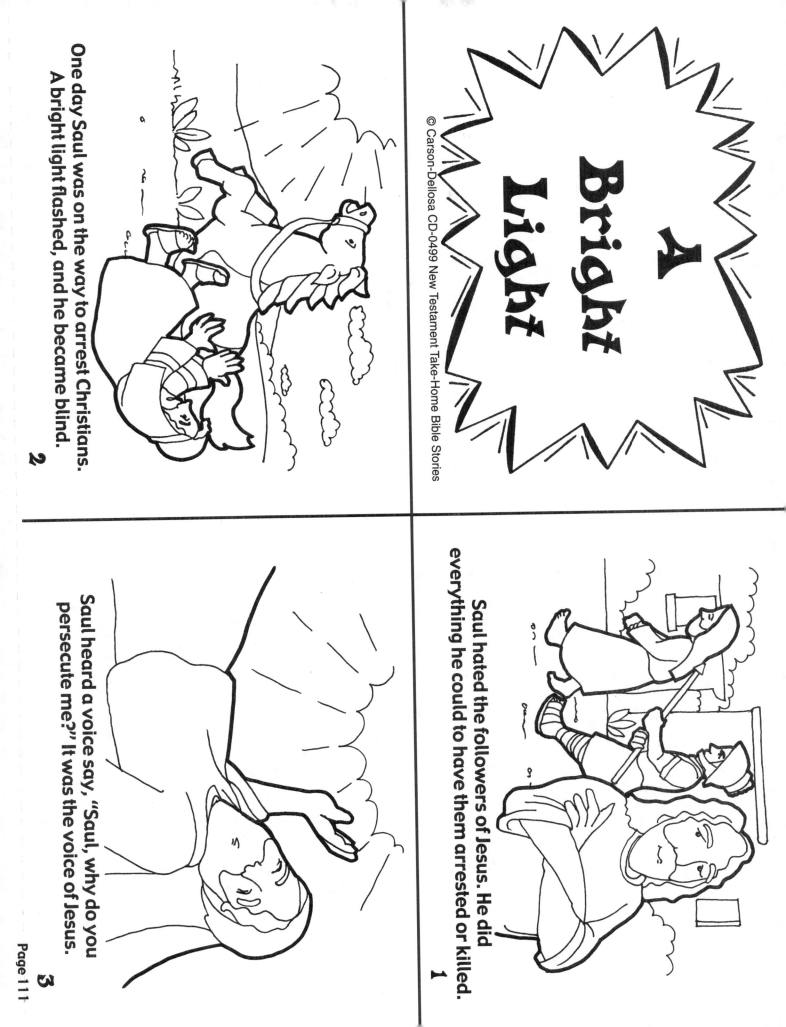

A Bright Light

One day Saul was on the way to arrest Christians. A bright light flashed, and he became blind.

2

Saul hated the followers of Jesus. He did everything he could to have them arrested or killed.

1

Saul heard a voice say, "Saul, why do you persecute me?" It was the voice of Jesus.

3

Jesus said, "I am Jesus, whom you are persecuting."

5

Why was Saul an unusual choice for an apostle?

Find this story in your Bible.
Acts 9:1

7

Saul had been blinded by the light and asked who was speaking to him.

4

Jesus told Saul to go to the city and wait. Saul was renamed Paul and became one of Jesus' greatest apostles.

6

Smuggling
Paul to Safety

1

Paul began to preach. People were amazed to hear love coming from a man who used to hate Christians.

2

Some people liked him better when he hated Christians.

3

They came up with a plan to hurt Paul and stop him from preaching.

They sneaked him out of the house. But the men who wanted to hurt Paul guarded the city gates.

5

Why did people want to hurt Paul?

Find this story in your Bible.
Acts 9:20

7

The men who were helping Paul heard about the plan. "You must leave the city immediately!"

4

The men lowered Paul over the city wall in a basket. Unseen by his enemies, Paul escaped to freedom.

6

Peter Escapes from Prison

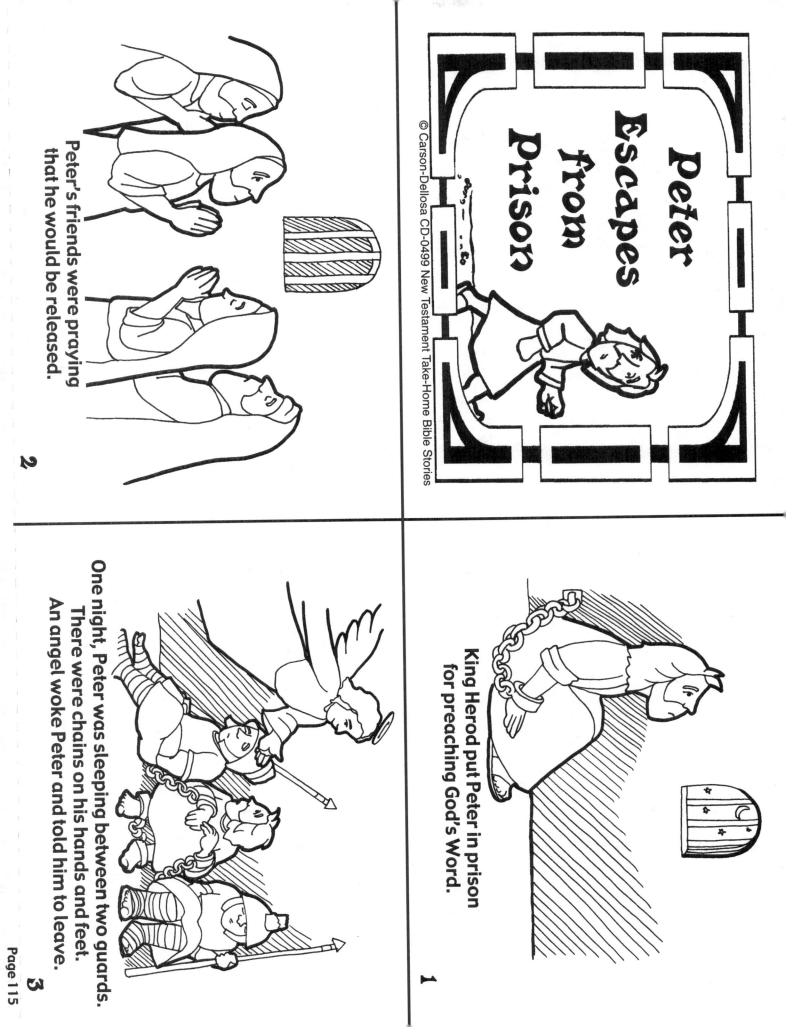

Peter's friends were praying that he would be released.

2

King Herod put Peter in prison for preaching God's word.

1

One night, Peter was sleeping between two guards. There were chains on his hands and feet. An angel woke Peter and told him to leave.

3

5

Peter went where his friends were praying. A woman opened the door and was so amazed to see him, she shut the door in his face.

7

How does having faith in God's love help you to respond to situations?

_____

_____

_____

_____

Find this story in your Bible.
Acts 12:1

4

The chains fell off. Peter left while the guards slept.

6

Later, they all rejoiced.

Paul and Silas in Prison

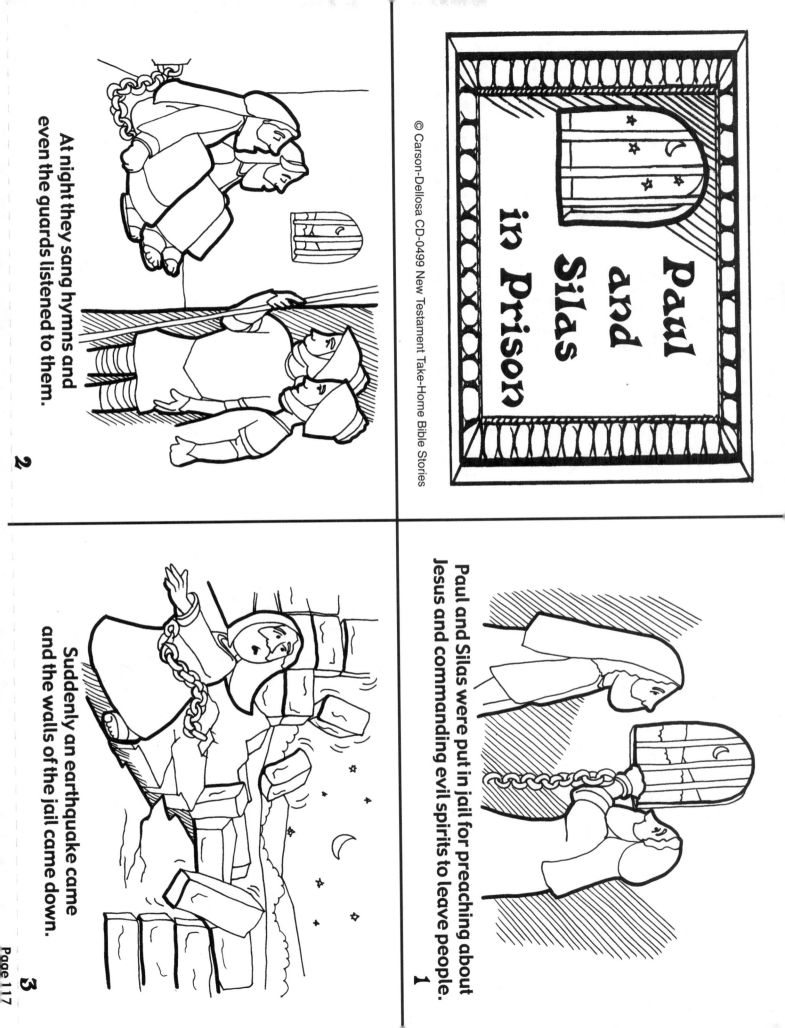

At night they sang hymns and even the guards listened to them.

2

Paul and Silas were put in jail for preaching about Jesus and commanding evil spirits to leave people.

1

Suddenly an earthquake came and the walls of the jail came down.

3

5

The frightened guard heard Paul say, "We're still here." The guard was amazed and asked, "How can I be saved?" Paul and Silas told him about Jesus.

7

When are good times to sing songs to God?

Find this story in your Bible.
Acts 16:16

4

One guard thought Paul and Silas had escaped. He knew that he could be killed if a prisoner escaped.

6

The guard wanted his whole family to know, so he brought Paul and Silas to his house.

Man in the Window

When midnight came he was still preaching. Candles lighted the room.

2

Paul was preaching a very important message to the people of Troas. Paul spoke to them in an upper room of a house. He spoke all day and into the night.

1

A man listening by the window fell asleep and then fell out the window.

3

5

Paul held him and said, "There's life in him." The man breathed.

7

How long could you talk about God before you ran out of things to say?

Find this story in your Bible.
Acts 20:7

4

Everyone ran down and found him dead.

6

Everyone went back upstairs. Paul continued to preach until the sun came up.

Nephew to the Rescue

The religious leaders decided he should be sent to Rome for a trial.

2

Paul was arrested in Jerusalem for preaching about Jesus to a big crowd.

1

A group of forty men decided they would not eat or drink until they killed Paul.

3

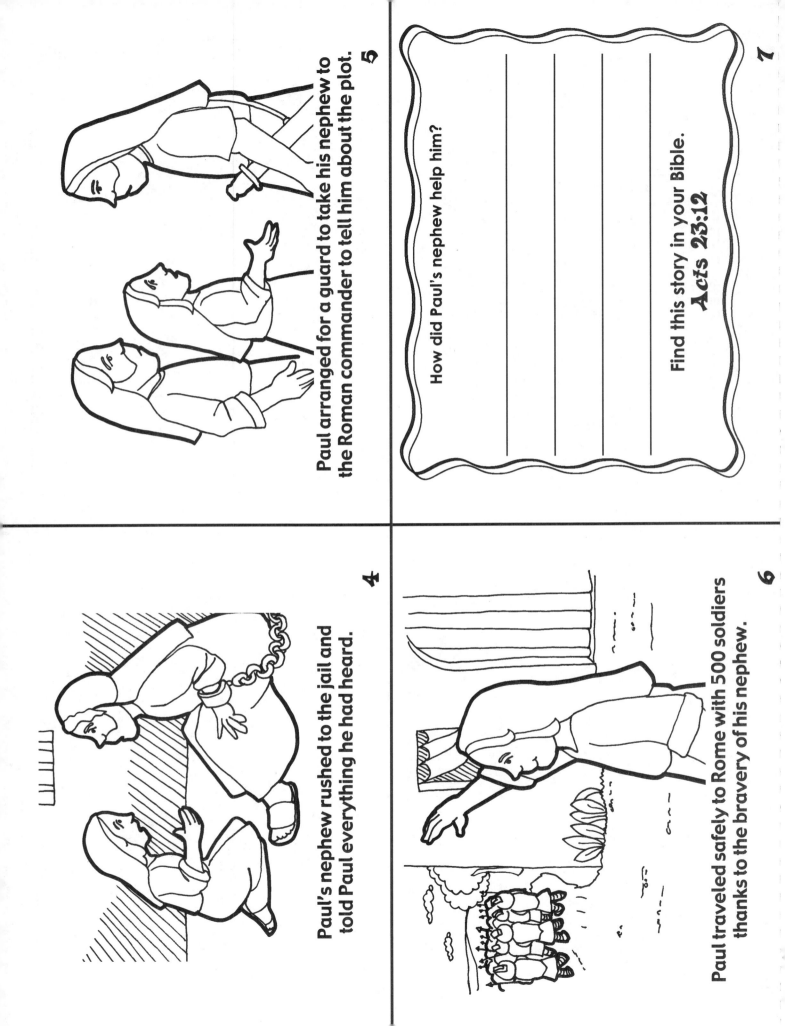

5

Paul arranged for a guard to take his nephew to the Roman commander to tell him about the plot.

7

How did Paul's nephew help him?

Find this story in your Bible.
Acts 23:12

4

Paul's nephew rushed to the jail and told Paul everything he had heard.

6

Paul traveled safely to Rome with 500 soldiers thanks to the bravery of his nephew.

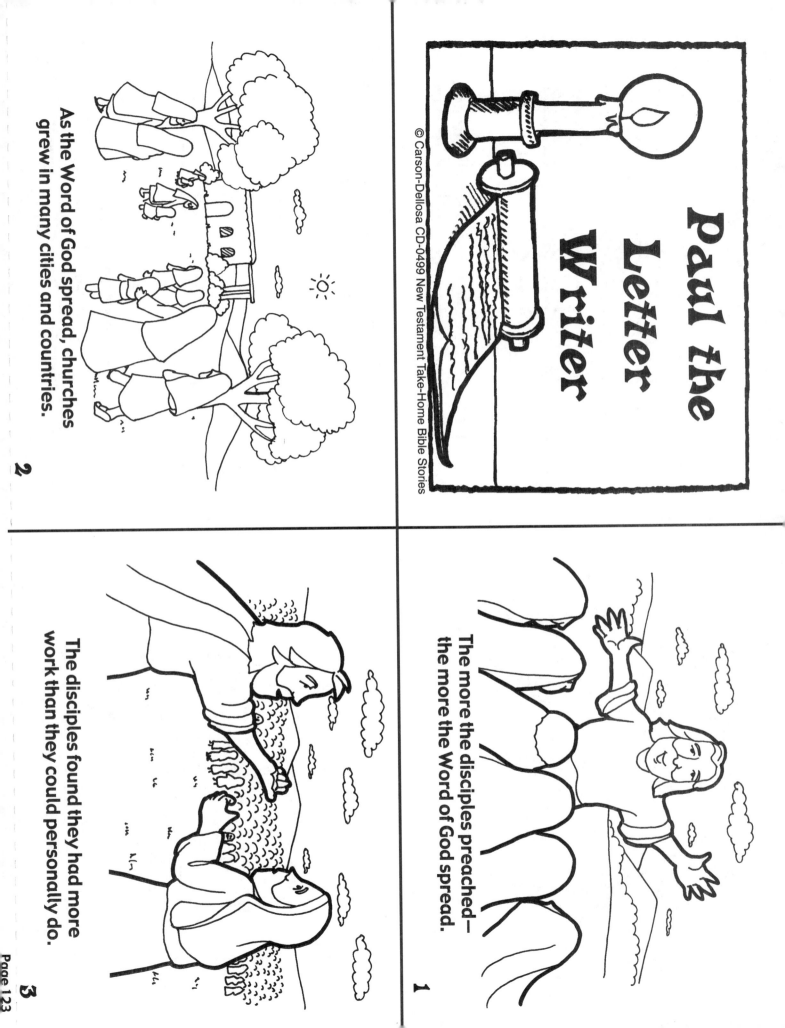

Paul the Letter Writer

© Carson-Dellosa CD-0499 New Testament Take-Home Bible Stories

As the Word of God spread, churches grew in many cities and countries.

2

The disciples found they had more work than they could personally do.

3

The more the disciples preached— the more the Word of God spread.

1

5

Paul sent many letters to the church leaders. He told them about God and how to run their churches.

7

Write a letter to someone to tell them about God.

Find this story in your Bible.
Romans 1:1

4

They baptized more believers, made more disciples, and sent them out to preach.

6

NEW TESTAMENT

Later these letters were gathered together and became part of the New Testament.

. . . Noah built the ark and saved his family . . . .

2

Heroes of Faith

Paul wrote a letter about faithful servants of God . . . .

1

. . . Abraham left his home to receive God's promises . . . .

3

ABRAHAM

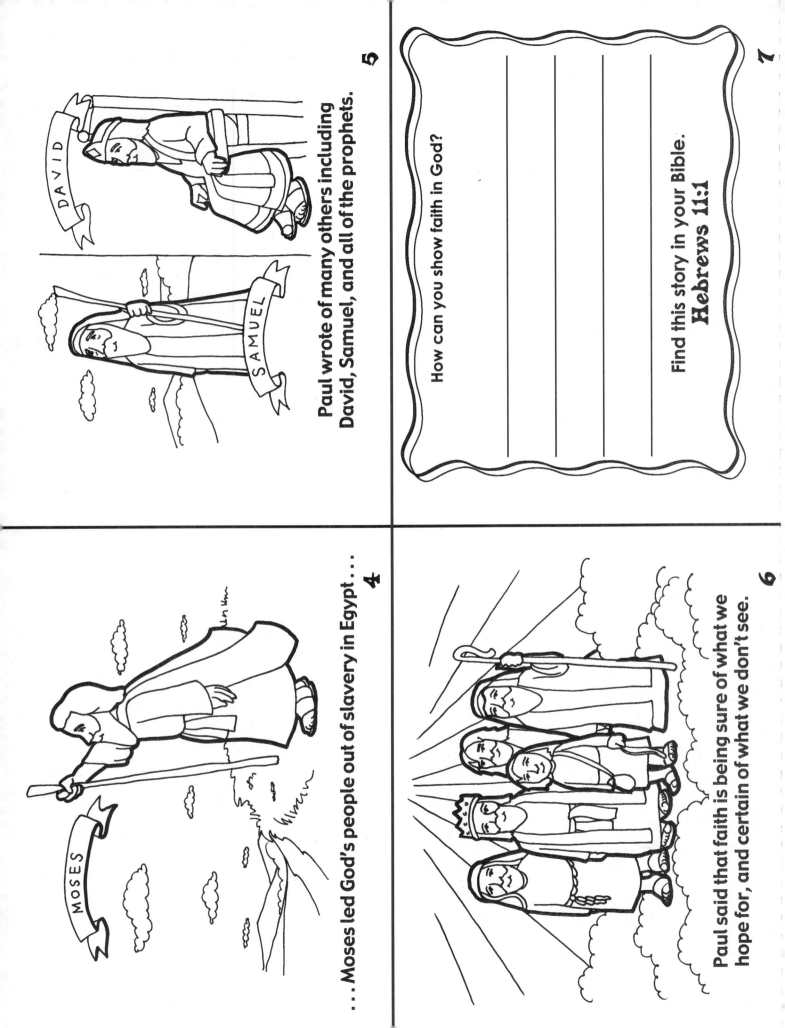

5

Paul wrote of many others including David, Samuel, and all of the prophets.

7

How can you show faith in God?

Find this story in your Bible.
Hebrews 11:1

4

. . . Moses led God's people out of slavery in Egypt . . .

6

Paul said that faith is being sure of what we hope for, and certain of what we don't see.

Jesus Is Coming Soon

While he was there, Jesus appeared to him with news that He wanted John to give to all of the churches.

2

John was sent to live on the island of Patmos as punishment for being one of Jesus' apostles.

1

He told John to write the churches and tell them to keep doing good things and stop doing bad things.

3

But He also told of how God would defeat Satan forever.

5

He told John about a time in the future when Satan would cause bad things to happen on earth.

4

Why can we be happy about the future?

_____
_____
_____
_____
_____

Find this story in your Bible.
Revelation 22:12

7

Jesus said, "I am coming soon." This was a promise telling us that, one day, we will see Jesus face to face.

6